LOVE YOURSELF, BE YOURSELF TO EMPOWER YOUR IMAGE

YOUR TEENS GUIDE TO GET RID OF YOUR INSECURITIES AND EMBRACE CONFIDENCE

GILL GRANT

© **Copyright 2023 - All rights reserved.**

The content contained within this book may not be reproduced, duplicated, or transmitted without direct written permission from the author or the publisher.

Under no circumstances will any blame or legal responsibility be held against the publisher, or author, for any damages, reparation, or monetary loss due to the information contained within this book, either directly or indirectly.

Legal Notice:

This book is copyright protected. It is only for personal use. You cannot amend, distribute, sell, use, quote, or paraphrase any part, or the content within this book, without the author or publisher's permission.

Disclaimer Notice:

Please note that the information contained within this document is for educational and entertainment purposes only. All effort has been executed to present accurate, up-to-date, reliable, complete information. No warranties of any kind are declared or implied. Readers acknowledge that the author is not rendering legal, financial, medical, or professional advice. The content within this book has been derived from various sources. Please consult a licensed professional before attempting any techniques outlined in this book.

By reading this document, the reader agrees that under no circumstances is the author responsible for any losses, direct or indirect, that are incurred due to the use of the information in this document, including, but not limited to, errors, omissions, or inaccuracies.

CONTENTS

About the Author … 7
Introduction … 9

1. UNDERSTANDING BODY AND SELF-IMAGE … 13
   Physical And Mental … 15

2. NEGATIVE THOUGHTS AND CHALLENGING THEM … 27
   What Are Negative Thoughts and Where Do They Come From? … 28

3. CULTIVATING SELF-CARE HABITS … 41
   Physical … 42

4. MINDFUL SELF-ACCEPTANCE … 57
   Mindfulness Techniques … 59

5. BUILDING HEALTHY RELATIONSHIPS … 69
   What Is a Healthy Relationship and What Is Not? … 70
   Exercises … 82

6. SELF-EXPRESSION AND CONFIDENCE … 85
   Creative Outlets … 87

7. PEER PRESSURE AND HOW SOCIAL MEDIA PLAYS A ROLE … 97
   The Power It Wields … 98

8. IT'S OKAY TO ASK FOR HELP … 113
   Know When to Speak Up … 114

BONUS CHAPTER	127
Inspirational Quotes	128
Conclusion	137
References	141

ABOUT THE AUTHOR

Allow me to introduce myself—I'm Gill Grant, a self-taught explorer of the human mind, and I'm on a mission to make a difference as a compassionate global traveler. At 52 years young, I believe in boundless energy and a deep well of empathy, qualities that have fueled my incredible journey.

While I spent many years studying psychology in traditional academic settings, I came to realize that genuine understanding doesn't solely come from books and lectures. It blossoms from immersing oneself in the diverse tapestry of human experiences across the world. This realization inspired me to embark on a unique path of self-discovery.

My travels have taken me from the bustling streets of New Delhi to the serene villages of Africa. In each place, I've rolled up my sleeves and worked alongside communities facing a multitude of challenges. Through my humanitarian missions, I've touched countless lives, leaving behind an indelible mark of empathy and support.

As a tireless advocate for personal growth and mental well-being, I transitioned from the academic world to a hands-on approach. My psychology background enables me to connect with individuals from all walks of life, providing me with profound insights into the complexities of the human psyche.

My approach to self-help is not just about offering advice; it's about fostering genuine connections and equipping individuals with the tools to navigate life's challenges with resilience and self-compassion. My warm and relatable style has resonated with people worldwide, transcending cultural boundaries.

I invite you to join me on this journey of self-help discovery, where every page is an invitation to embrace personal growth, mental well-being, and the boundless capacity of the human spirit. My message is clear: You have the power to transform your life, and I'm here as your guide, mentor, and friend on this incredible journey.

INTRODUCTION

If you have no confidence in self, you are twice defeated in the race of life. With confidence, you have won even before you have started.

— CICERO

Have you ever found yourself looking in the mirror and just not liking what you see? Maybe you're not particularly bothered with your actual looks, but something about yourself just makes you feel unworthy or inferior. Everyone has issues with self-esteem from time to time, but it's something that you need to actively work to overcome. If you are thinking that it's easier said than done, then you're absolutely right—but it can be done. And I am here to help guide you through it.

The journey of self-discovery and empowerment is more thrilling, challenging, and rewarding than ever before. But in a world that still has some kind of "ideal" of everything and everyone (in the 21st Century, you'd think they would have let go of that by now), it's also harder than ever. As a teenager, you find yourself at a unique crossroads of transformation, poised to become the very best version of yourself. But there is also the option of navigating down the wrong path and that's not what we want. The idea of loving and accepting yourself is not just a notion but a powerful reality. One you need to grab onto!

As you stand on the threshold of adolescence, you're about to uncover the magic of being unapologetically yourself. It's a journey through the intricacies of navigating society's standards, building unbreakable self-esteem, challenging negative thoughts, and practicing self-care with tender, loving kindness.

It's an opportunity to discover the power of your voice, to express yourself authentically, and to face down the challenges of peer pressure and social media influences with courage and resilience.

As a psychologist with many years of experience, I know that there is much more to loving and accepting yourself and that you may need a little help sometimes. That's okay! We're here to help, and even though I may not be able to help you in person physically, there are many other mental health professionals who would love to help you because that's what we do!

As a parent, I've also supported my kids through their teenage years, and hey, I was a teenager, too! But what really inspired this book is the fact that I work with so many young people daily, and seeing how much self-confidence can negatively affect them is heartbreaking.

At the same time, seeing how positively more self-confidence can affect them is absolutely amazing. You will be surprised at the transformation that can take place in your life if you gain a little more confidence!

You should not have to change yourself in order to "fit in," and you shouldn't have to want to.

In this book, you can expect to learn about some points that will help you get where you need to be. But beyond that, I've also added some pointers and a few small activities that you can try as well.

We'll delve into self-esteem, explore the complex web of societal expectations, and navigate the labyrinth of self-care. It's an exploration of mindfulness that will allow you to savor every moment and accept what you can't change. You'll also learn the importance of setting boundaries in your relationships, a skill that will empower you in your interactions with others.

Your voice is powerful; you just need to find it. This book will hopefully also help you discover your strength against the pressures of peer influence and the ever-present world of social media. You'll find the resilience to stay true to yourself and face these challenges head-on.

Are you ready to challenge the "norm" and learn to love yourself? If your answer is yes, then let's not waste another moment.

UNDERSTANDING BODY AND SELF-IMAGE

I'm one of the world's most self-conscious people. I really have to struggle.

— MARILYN MONROE

The curtains open, and bright lights flash in your face; the stage is full of young people who are putting on the performance of their lives. Except it's not a stage, and there are no flashing lights. The crowd is still there, though, criticizing your every move.

When did life become a performance? When did the crowd's cheer become so important that we would do or believe anything for it?

Marilyn Monroe was considered to be one of the most beautiful women in history. A literal crowd was cheering for her every step of the way, yet she openly admitted to being self-conscious.

If someone like that has struggled with body image and self-confidence, then it's reassuring to know that we can, too. This isn't limited to young women alone, as even individuals like the renowned Dwayne "The Rock" Johnson have admitted to feeling self-conscious about themselves. It's remarkable to imagine that someone society considers the "ultimate" male specimen (an outdated term, but society often creates its own standards) also experienced similar feelings, particularly during his younger years.

The unfortunate reality? Every single person has something that they feel self-conscious about. I find it difficult to believe that anyone goes through life thinking that they're perfect and their bodies are perfect. What does that tell us? That, my friends, tells us that we are not alone.

PHYSICAL AND MENTAL

One of the most common misconceptions is that being self-confident, or self-conscious for that matter, is all about the way you look. In fact, it's about how you see yourself, which does not always relate to your physical form.

Take mental health, for example; many people are ashamed of their mental health status or medication when they really shouldn't be.

There are numerous reasons for feeling inadequate, but the truth is that it doesn't define you. How you perceive yourself may not align with how others perceive you. You may think of yourself as the boy who never grew as tall as the others, while your friends might think of you as the clever one, or the musician, or the funny one, or whatever the heck else. Body dysmorphia could play a role in something like this, but that's a topic we'll cover a little later on.

We're Not Born This Way

Feeling like you're not good enough isn't a natural phenomenon, though it's so common that it may feel that way. Think about a toddler happily playing with their friends in the sandbox. Do they seem self-conscious? Probably not, even if they might actually visibly be different from the other kids. That's because it isn't something that we're born with, just like hate, racism, and all the other negativities in the world. It's taught, not natural.

That's a good thing, you know, because it means that even though we may have our doubts and negativities, since it isn't in our nature, we can change it. That's right; you're not doomed. You've got this.

The Damage It Does

Negative self-perception can significantly affect your life. Constantly criticizing yourself or harboring negative thoughts can impact your social interactions. Have you ever experienced reluctance to attend school functions or social gatherings due to self-consciousness?

That is the first step to social isolation, which, if you don't know is actually bad. As human beings, we're social "creatures" who need each other. But that's not the only reason; social interaction and positive relationships are necessary for our mental health.

The fact is, even if you may not believe it, negative self-perception can lead to mental health illnesses such as depression, anxiety/social anxiety, eating disorders, and more. It's like a domino effect; you flip one over, and the whole thing comes tumbling down.

Why? Because if you're not your biggest fan, then it does not matter how many or how few other "fans" you might have.

Body Image

Unfortunately, a big part of your self-confidence might actually come from how you perceive yourself physically. It means that you're not happy with how you look. When that is the case, you may have some of the following "symptoms."

- constantly comparing yourself to others
- not liking the sight of yourself in the mirror
- feeling ashamed of your appearance for whatever reason
- not indulging in the simple pleasures of life for fear of being seen or weight gain/loss
- not eating in front of other people
- over-exercising or not exercising enough for fear of being mocked by others

And, of course, many, many more. Feel free to take a piece of paper and continue with the list. Don't just think about physical things for this little activity. Think about everything that makes you feel bad about yourself or that you don't like and write it down. Then, write down the negative impacts that they have on your life.

When you look at it all on paper, it brings a different kind of reality check, doesn't it? You need to take your time when performing this activity, even if it takes more than a day.

Social Media and Society

I'd say it's almost worse, the way social media is now. I could look at myself in the mirror and think, 'Wow, I'm ugly.' And I could look at a picture of me from the same day and go, 'I look like I'm having so much fun.

— BILLIE EILISH

You know, social media, at its core, is not a bad thing. Many people paint it as evil these days, but just like money (supposedly the root of all evil), it can absolutely be used for good. The original idea was to be able to connect people across the oceans and to remove barriers that kept us from staying in touch with each other. It was meant to bring friends, family, and people all over the world closer to one another. That, in and of itself, is not a bad thing. Social media is very handy for people who travel for work, or need to move far away, or even when you need to pop your sibling a text to tell them that they need to stop hogging the hot water.

But unfortunately, social media has evolved into much more than simply a means of communication. Now, there are thousands of platforms where we can share just about anything, again, not necessarily needing to be a bad thing. But, people have made it into the negativity that it is today.

When I was younger, magazines already influenced us and how we felt about ourselves very heavily, but there was a pretty easy solution: don't buy them and look away. It's not so easy to "look away" when you're faced with society's standards every time you touch your phone.

It's not even the celebrities anymore; it's the everyday people. With the evolution of technology, it has now become possible for every Tom, Dick, and Harry to be able to edit their photos to such an extent that they become unrecognizable to the people who know them personally. Sure, I can see how the need to feel better about yourself might drive a person to such lengths. But when you really think about it, by altering pictures so much, you would be doing what society has done to you. Others would see these artificial images and take them for reality, leading to further self-loathing and a vicious cycle that never ends.

Another risk factor is that many people's insecurities drive them far beyond artificial alterations. Mental health disorders, including eating disorders, are legitimate and critical conditions that must be taken seriously. Contrary to popular belief, they also don't only affect girls or women; men are just as affected.

While reading this, it's important to remember that if you identify as male, your feelings are just as valid as anyone else's. Men are not always as vocal as women about their inner struggles, and that leads to what we know today as "toxic masculinity" because society would have us believe that men are not supposed to cry, have feelings, or have any issues other than obvious physical ailments.

"He broke his leg? Poor guy, we should send him a text."

"He's depressed? Ah, shoot. Man up!"

That, my friends, is toxic.

I knew a young man who was brilliant in every way you can think of. Good grades, considered "handsome," funny, and kind. However, he wasn't exactly as tall as the other guys in his class. While many of his peers didn't make a big deal out of it, it was a big deal to him because of the few who did and because of the "ideal male" picture.

It was a hardship that pulled at him for most of his life, severely affecting his social life and more. I ask you this: Is it worth sacrificing your social life and your happiness for something that others want you to have?

It's not! The people who care about you care about you just the way you are. The actionable step that you need to take here is to block out the negative and focus on the positive. Yes, yes, that's absolutely easier said than done, but it's possible.

You need to focus on the things that you do have instead.

For example, stand in front of your mirror every day, look at yourself, and count your blessings. You can see, hear, touch, smell, smile, walk, and much more. You are blessed. And even if you do have a physical or mental disability, you still have other things that you can be grateful for.

I know everyone tells you to start a gratitude journal. It sounds old-fashioned, but hey, take it from me, it works. Besides, you can't discard something until you have actually tried it for yourself!

How You See Yourself

What truly baffles my mind is that we would believe the words of random strangers over the people who truly care about us. Think about it: How we see ourselves, as mentioned before, is not a reflection of how we're born; it's what we're taught. Take a kitten raised by a mother dog. It will spend its life believing that it's a dog, just like the other puppies, until someone tells it differently.

This is a somewhat primitive example, but it explains the point well. You will grow up and live a normal (whatever that means to you), happy life without ever considering that you might be different until someone points it out.

The sad truth is that in the ideal world, there would be nobody who points out supposed flaws or differences or paints unrealistic ideals. But we don't live in the perfect world. In this very flawed world, there will always be someone who tries to dim your light. And that, dear friends, is very often where our perception of ourselves comes from—from others.

With this being such a built-in factor, what can we actually do about it? For starters, we can work toward rewiring our brains This preset function that was carved into our minds needs to be wiped away, and we need to learn to love ourselves.

Next, let's go through a series of steps that you can start with to help you see yourself in a new light.

When someone has something negative to say about you, be "that" person who smiles at them, laughs, and walks away. You see, bullies are often taken aback when we don't react as emotionally as they want us to. It may sound silly, but give it a try. You might just be pleasantly surprised.

Now, remember that even if you shrug it off in public, it might still hurt. It's important to acknowledge your feelings and to take the time you need to process them. But whatever you do, remember that the person who hurt you was actively trying to hurt you. It doesn't mean that there is any truth to what they said.

See, when you really think about it, it's rather sad that bullies exist in the first place. They are either insecure themselves, have gone through traumatic experiences, or, yes, as your Gran told you in kindergarten, they might actually just be "jealous" of you. It's very easy to attack someone emotionally when they flourish.

So, the next thing you can try is to actually be kind. You know how they always say that we need to be the better people, and we need to turn the other cheek? Well, sometimes that actually is what is necessary. If a bully is insecure or has gone through or is going through their own trauma, they might just need a little kindness.

The next tip is to believe the people who care about you when they give you compliments or say nice things about you. I know, it's almost an instinctive reaction to say something along the lines of "Oh, you don't mean that," but don't do that! Even if you really don't believe them, go ahead and respond with a "thank you" instead. By accepting the compliments, you're subconsciously programming yourself to accept them more easily and frequently. When you accept them, you might just start believing it.

It's a Material World

See, another thing to consider is that the world is very "money driven." Many of the people we look up to need a significant amount of money to pay for their skincare, makeup, gym equipment/memberships, special diets, photo editors, and much more. Yes, natural beauties are real. But a lot of what we see is actually "hidden ads."

Our whole world is filled with ads for different products, treatments, places, and more. There is nothing wrong with pampering yourself or changing something if you don't like it (absolutely not necessary; you're perfect the way you are), but it's a thought to consider the next time you look at photos of people on social media or on television. Or even when you look at people you know, don't fall into the trap of being envious of people for things they have or even for how they look. It's tempting and not easy to miss when everyone seems to have it easier than you do, but it's called a trap for a reason. If you're going to hyper-fixate on anything, let it be on being a better person, your health, and your future.

Conclusion

In a world where the lines between what is real and what is not are extremely blurred, don't let society's ideas get you down. You are perfect the way you are, you have a whole lot to be grateful for, and you can absolutely start rewiring your brain today, not tomorrow!

If you can start by not taking bullies seriously, showing some kindness, and actually accepting the compliments given to you, you might just get there sooner rather than later.

Remember, we're not born with insecurities; they are taught. Just like those "memes" you may have seen about hate being taught, hey, it's the same concept. Nobody is born hating anything, not even themselves. That comes with outside influences.

But unfortunately, as pretty as it all sounds, our own minds are often our greatest enemies. Negative thoughts can be crippling and damaging to our mental and physical health, not to mention the quality of our actual lives. So, in the next chapter, we're going to talk about challenging these negative thoughts and conquering them. If we can deal with outside criticism, we can deal with our insides, too.

2

NEGATIVE THOUGHTS AND CHALLENGING THEM

To build self-esteem, you have to outface your negative beliefs about yourself and change them

— ASMAA DOKMAK

Negative thoughts can be crippling, and the truth is that they are not even real. Picture yourself as the main character of a movie or a book; every good one has some form of negativity that the main character needs to overcome. In many cases, it can be some kind of villain. In this case, negative thoughts=villain. And we're about to kick its a**.

WHAT ARE NEGATIVE THOUGHTS AND WHERE DO THEY COME FROM?

"Negative thoughts" is a pretty simple term. If we want to get a little more technical, we can call them "cognitive distortions" (Cuncic, 2020). When we address the issue by a more scientific name, it's often taken more seriously. That should not be the case, but unfortunately, in many cases, it is. Not everyone will take negative thoughts seriously; they're just thoughts, right? We can simply change them or stop them, right? Not necessarily. They can affect every single aspect of your life, you guessed it, negatively.

You might wonder how your thoughts can actually impact your life. Well, it's not an old wives tale; everything is actually linked in some way. Think it, do it. This can be a positive "motto" if you use it the right way.

Big contributors to having negative thoughts are high pressure from family, peers, social media, and more. As discussed in Chapter 1, social media can often lead to issues regarding your self-esteem, and at the core of your self-esteem are your thoughts. Your internal monologue is how you talk to yourself in your head, and while not everyone has this, most people do. Your monologue can be positive or negative as well, and that's one of the biggest villains we will ever face: ourselves. When you constantly criticize yourself, your negative thoughts are bound to blossom.

Negative thoughts, or cognitive distortions, come in many different forms. One of the most well-known forms of negative thoughts is known as "labeling" (Outreach, 2021). In my opinion, labeling kind of leads to the others; it's like the first step.

According to Sandra Silva Casabianca (2021), there are 15 common cognitive distortions, namely:

- filtering
- jumping to conclusions
- polarization
- overgeneralization
- catastrophizing
- discounting the positive
- personalization
- control fallacies
- fallacy of fairness
- fallacy of change
- blaming
- "shoulds"

- global labeling
- emotional reasoning
- always being right (Casabianca, 2021).

Labeling was mentioned by Casabianca as "global labeling," and it's another common cognitive distortion. The reason why I believe that labeling is important is because when you label yourself as something, it tends to affect your entire thought pattern.

When you label yourself as unworthy of praise or affection, that directly affects how you think and what you do. You won't go for that love interest because you don't deserve their affection, for example. This can start the cycle of other negative thoughts.

Let's briefly discuss each of the other 15 and what they mean.

- Filtering refers to when you focus only on the negativity.
- Jumping to conclusions is all about making negative assumptions.
- Polarization is when you only see things as all good or all bad, with no gray area.

- Overgeneralization refers to making conclusions based on a few things that may have happened. For example, if you lose one contest, then assume that you will lose every time.
- Catastrophizing is always expecting the worst possible outcome in a situation.
- Discounting the positive is belittling or ignoring positive experiences or qualities, similar to filtering.
- Personalization is taking things too personally.
- Control fallacies are either feeling helpless, like everything is out of your control or believing you have complete control over everything.
- The fallacy of fairness is expecting the world to treat you fairly when, unfortunately, we live in a very unfair world.
- The fallacy of change is basically expecting everything and everyone to change to meet your needs.
- Blaming is simply described as blaming others for anything that might go wrong in your life, even if you might actually be to blame.

- "Shoulds" refers to imposing rigid expectations on yourself or others.
- Global labeling is using extreme words to describe yourself or others based on limited behaviors, which we have already discussed.
- Emotional reasoning is believing that because you feel a certain way, it must be true.
- Always being right is believing that you're, well, as the name suggests, always right.

It's very easy to get lost in these thought patterns because it's often easier to criticize yourself rather than compliment yourself. For some reason, the world kind of looks down on people who "toot their own horns," which I find ridiculous. Are you good at sports? Toot it! A fantastic pianist? Toot away! And it doesn't have to be talents or accomplishments alone. You're allowed to feel good about yourself for any level of accomplishment. Did you get out of bed without snoozing the alarm today? You bet that's an accomplishment you can be proud of.

The point is, all this negative thinking doesn't benefit you in any way. Remember how we mentioned that unfair world? Well, it's not very nice and it'll throw more than enough negativity at you.

There is no logical reason for you to further the negativity in your own life.

It's easier said than done; once again, I understand that. Especially if you may not have the most supportive structure around you it can be hard to try and be "nice" to yourself when everyone around you doesn't exactly help in that regard.

How They Affect You and What You Can Do

As mentioned before, these thoughts can affect us in different ways. The most obvious way it affects you is by increasing different kinds of anxiety, as well as depression (Scott, 2022).

This can lead to decreases in your productivity, motivation, and social life. When you feel depressed, you might not exactly have the motivation to work as hard in school as you usually do or to spend as much time with friends and family. In turn, this leads to even further feelings of depression as self-isolation gets worse and your grades start slipping.

It's a vicious cycle that doesn't stop as the dominoes fall one by one, triggering the others as they go. When you find yourself in such a spiral, it can be difficult to see a way out, but I assure you. There is one.

You need to challenge your negative thoughts, and you need to change your mindset. Firstly, you need to look at the 15 types of negative thinking above and address them individually. Do you relate to any of them? It's okay to admit it; in fact, admitting it is the first step in the right direction.

Write each of them down, and take some time to think about instances where you may have had thoughts that correlate with them. Once you've got them, the difficult part begins.

You need to recognize that there were better ways to handle each of those situations or thoughts. I want you to think about how you could have handled it better or what you could have replaced those negative thoughts with. Replacing negative thoughts with positive ones is a very helpful strategy in dealing with the intrusion.

Here is an example:

Negative thought	What can I replace it with?
I labeled myself as someone who isn't good with sports, so I didn't try out for the football team, even though I actually really wanted to.	Okay, so maybe I didn't do that well with other sports, but I like football, and I won't know if I don't try. And even if I'm not great at it, I can work toward being great!
The teacher made a remark about how some students could really need those extra math classes. They were probably talking about me but didn't want to say it to me directly.	I could benefit from some extra classes since my last test didn't go so well. The teacher is considerate by offering extra classes for all students who need them.
I hate my nose; everyone probably looks at it all the time. My nose enters the room before I do.	I'm perfect just the way I am. It's okay to not like every inch of my body, but it's not okay to hate anything about myself. Nobody is hyper-fixating on my nose the way I am. They'll notice my sense of humor instead.
I stood up for my friend when they were bullied, but they didn't stand up for me. I'm never helping anyone again.	I stood up for my friend because it was the right thing to do, and even if they didn't stand up for me, the world isn't always fair. And they might have been too scared to do anything about it. I need to continue being the best version of myself that I can be.
I'll never be a dancer because of my weight.	My weight doesn't define me or my talents.
I'm too short, and girls don't like short guys.	The right girl will like me for more than my height.
My friends are not even really my friends; they just tolerate me because they don't want to be mean.	My friends like me for who I am, and even if I feel sad or bad about myself today, that doesn't mean that how they feel changes. Just because I think it doesn't make it true and I shouldn't assume the feelings of others.

My name was called over the intercom at school. I need to go to the principal's office. Oh, here we go, that's it. I'm finished; I knew I shouldn't have taken the last open seat in art class.	I was called into the principal's office. I'm nervous but I will not expect the worst to happen; I know I didn't do anything wrong.
My life sucks, and everyone around me is to blame because they just don't understand me.	My life doesn't suck, but I might be in a "sucky" situation right now; it will pass. It's not their fault that they don't understand me. I can try harder to help others understand how I feel while still taking into account how they feel.
I got second place in the race. I can't believe I didn't win. I'm a real loser.	I got second place! It might not be first place, but I still got a silver medallion, and it was a victory nonetheless!

These might be silly examples, but you can input your own and give it some real thought. For every negative thought, there is a more logical or more positive thought that we can replace it with.

It's not just about replacing negative thoughts. When you challenge them, you're looking them in the face and telling them that they don't make sense and they are not valid. It doesn't make sense to think that everyone hates you or that you're the worst singer in the whole world because they absolutely don't, and you're definitely not.

When we get overwhelmed with negativity, we sometimes need the old "slap in the face" to "snap out of it." But please, no literal slapping.

By a slap in the face, I mean a wake-up call. The activity above is a great way to sort of snap yourself out of the dark hole because it forces you to think outside of the box. Not only does it actually distract you from your negative feelings, but it puts emphasis on the positive.

There are other ways to challenge them, too, for example, by reminding yourself that some forms of constructive criticism are good. None of us would get anywhere if everyone told us we were amazing at everything, even though we pretty clearly are not.

That's why we need to learn to deal with it and *not take it personally.* The thing with criticism is that there is a very fine line between the good and the bad kind. And all it takes is one word to change the entire tone of the statement. And hey, here we go again; the world isn't fair. So, the criticism you get won't always be great or constructive. But you need to be able to take it and "shake it off" or learn from it. While you're at it, don't forget that for every kindness that you practice on yourself, you need to practice on others, too. If someone asks you how their dancing was, and they literally just flopped around like a clown, what do you say? Not that they flopped around like a clown, for sure.

You say something constructive and kind, yet honest, such as "You could use a little more practice but you're getting so much better! You've really improved since the last time I saw you."

It is helpful to mention that if you're not exactly an expert on something, you probably should not be criticizing it though. Remember, just because you don't like their dancing or someone's painting doesn't necessarily mean it's bad. It's okay to respond with, "I don't know enough about A, B, or C to really give you my opinion."

Body Dysmorphia

More specifically, some people don't necessarily have negative thoughts about their abilities but exclusively about their appearance. It's very much like what we've discussed so far, but body dysmorphia is a little more serious than just a thought.

When you hyper-fixate on a physical "flaw," no matter how big or small (it could be as small as a little beauty spot), and you obsess over it and convince yourself others do too, that's body dysmorphia (Mayo Clinic, 2022).

It's much more intense than feeling a little self-conscious over something that you may not particularly like. It's a crippling obsession that can take hours out of your day, to the point where you may be spending half your day trying to conceal whatever the issue is. Some people even go as far as not taking part in social activities and more because of their "flaws."

It's important to challenge this kind of thinking because, yes, it's not all about you! You're going to walk into school tomorrow, and chances are that most students won't even notice you enough to actually notice whatever your flaw is. But the most important thing here is to ask for help. If you think that you might be suffering from body dysmorphia, you need to reach out for professional help. While there are many guidelines and tips that can be shared regarding how to deal with mental illness, it's always best to consult with a professional first.

In our final chapter, we'll discuss knowing when to ask for help and how you can go about getting the help you need.

Getting the help you need is a form of self-care, you know. But there are other forms of self-care, too, and one of the most important parts of your "human experience" is taking care of yourself, both physically and mentally.

In the next chapter, we'll discuss encouraging healthy lifestyle choices that prioritize physical, emotional, and mental well-being.

I'm my own competition - I'm competing with myself. I'm not worried about the next girl. I'm focused on being the best version of me.

— LIZZO

3

CULTIVATING SELF-CARE HABITS

I'm too busy working on my own grass to notice if yours is greener.

— ANONYMOUS

Regardless of your age, self-care is essential. No, I'm not talking about eating an entire tub of ice cream because you've had a bad day. I'm talking about true self-care that will benefit your physical, emotional, and mental well-being.

You only have one body and one mind. So, take care of it! Don't be like the infamous Captain Jack Sparrow: "Nobody move! I dropped me brain."

PHYSICAL

A psychiatrist once explained it very well, and you might have heard this as well. Your well-being is like a chair; each leg plays a crucial part in keeping the chair standing. Three of the legs are your emotional, physical, and mental well-being. And the fourth is your support system (we'll discuss positive relationships later).

Without one, the chair falls. I often say that it's a good idea to begin with the physical aspect. Because looking after yourself physically leads to feeling good about yourself, more energy, lessened depression and anxiety, and overall, it's a positive cycle that begins with getting up and moving!

When we talk about our physical health, the most common thing that comes to mind is exercise. And while that's a crucial part of it, it's not the only important thing about your body that you need to worry about.

Health Challenge

Some of you might be pretty active already, taking part in sports and exercises of your own. But some of you might be like me, and you might not exactly "like" getting "physical." Well, whether we like it or not, we "gotta" do it.

I challenge every reader to the following "health" challenge, no matter your fitness level. Challenging yourself and actually using the word "challenge" is a great way to motivate yourself. And when you do reach that goal, it feels great. Keep in mind that it's important to keep to reasonable goals, especially if you're new at this!

This will be a ten-day challenge, five weekdays. That's it. While I like starting new things on Mondays, it's crucial to remember that the "I'll start on Monday" mindset can be damaging. Monday never comes, and neither does tomorrow or next week, in many cases. So, your start day definitely does not have to be a Monday. Start today, even if you're halfway through the day!

DAY	CHALLENGE
1	Start with any stretches you like first thing in the morning. Aim for at least 10,000 steps. This should be your daily step count and will be done along with different challenges for each day.
2	Remember your stretches and steps. Do five push-ups.
3	Remember your stretches and steps. Do five sit-ups.
4	Remember your stretches and steps. Plank for a minute.
5	Remember your stretches and steps. Ten squats.
6	Remember your stretches and steps. Ten Burpees, ten sit-ups.
7	Remember your stretches and steps. Ten push-ups, ten sit-ups, five squats.
8	Remember your stretches and steps. Ten squats, one minute plank, ten burpees, ten jumping jacks.
9	Remember your stretches and steps. Ten jumping jacks, run in one place for five minutes at max speed, ten squats, go up and down any stairs you can find, at least three times.
10	Remember your stretches and steps. Repeat day nine, and add a one-minute plank.

Keep in mind that it's likely a good idea to ensure that you can do these exercises by talking to your doctor first. This might sound like an easy challenge, and for some, it might just be, but for others, it won't be that easy! By challenging yourself, you can show yourself that you can indeed do it, and nothing is stopping you from repeating the challenge again or taking part in other sports.

There is nothing quite like a post-workout shower/bath. That's why I always recommend that you don't skip it! In fact, swimming is a great form of exercise and a great way to cool down after a workout. So, if you have access to a pool, don't be afraid to swim a few laps before your shower/bath.

Cleanliness

Another part of keeping your physical self healthy is something that some people might not really consider to be a part of your health, but let me assure you, it is! Good personal hygiene is crucial for your social life, if you know what I mean! But it's not only that; being conscious of your hygiene helps protect you from viruses and bacteria (which could obviously influence your mental and physical health).

Back in the olden days, doctors would actually even prescribe baths for certain ailments, and foul odors were associated with sickness. Of course, they were a little oblivious to bacteria and viruses back then, but they did kind of have a point when it came to bad odors.

Taking a bath or shower first thing in the morning helps us feel more awake and fresh for the day, while taking a bath at night could promote a better night's sleep. From personal experience, I can say that there is nothing quite like hopping into bed after a warm shower.

Now, similar to bathing being prescribed for some physical ailments in the olden days, bathing is often also advised for the benefit of your mental health. I don't believe that there is much scientific evidence behind it, but I will admit that a negative situation feels a little better after a bit of a soak.

Keeping your personal hygiene on point also helps with your self-esteem, which is critical for your well-being. As you can see, it's a good idea to grab some soap and water, and don't forget to wash behind your ears!

What we also often forget about is skin care as well, and no boys, this isn't just for the girls. Boys will absolutely also benefit from a good skin cleanser, some exfoliation, and a good moisturizer.

Don't fall for the toxic masculinity stunts stating that men who use skin care products are not manly enough; that's a load of nonsense. You only have one skin, and you'll have it for the rest of your days.

Eating A Balanced Diet

Another important thing that you might not always think about is your eating habits. Yes, yes, we hear it all the time. Eat your veggies, don't have too much sugar, blah blah. But let me tell you, it's more serious than it sounds. When you're young, the negative effects of what you eat might not really show up just yet, but they'll catch up with you.

Although, I will say that having too much sugar and fatty, processed foods can lead to bad skin breakouts. It's important to note that there is nothing that you *have* to cut out of your diet, but as my grandfather always said, moderation is key. You can enjoy (almost) anything in life moderately.

Example of a good daily meal plan:

Meal Time	Foods
Breakfast	Oatmeal with honey and sliced fruits/yogurt
Snack	A handful of nuts
Lunch	Steamed chicken breast served on full grain bread with lettuce, tomato, and seasoning of choice
Snack	Banana
Dinner	Roast beef with mashed potatoes, green beans, a green salad, and some gravy
Snack/dessert	One cup of vanilla ice cream with chocolate sauce
Before bed	Sliced apple

The above is once again a simple example, and you'll need to work with your parents and possibly your doctor in order to work out the right diet for you. But it does show you that you can have sweet things, and while modern social media will tell you to cut starchy foods out completely, you don't have to. It does need to be limited, though.

And you're also able to ensure that your portions are enough to keep you going but not too big. They say that having smaller meals more frequently is better for you, so go ahead and give that a try.

When we eat healthy, we feel more energized and overall healthier. It also helps to not feel so bloated all the time!

Another part of feeling refreshed and energized is getting enough sleep, which brings us to our next topic.

Sleep

The average teenager needs between eight and ten hours of sleep per night (CDC, 2020). While you could probably function on less sleep, it would not be a good idea in the long run. Getting enough sleep is probably one of the most important parts of self-care. It promotes both physical and mental well-being.

Tips for better sleep:

- Avoid caffeine.
- Avoid any blue light devices (cellphones, laptops, TV, etc.) at least two hours before bed.
- Try reading before bed (this always makes me sleepy!).

- Don't eat a large meal too close to bed (a sliced apple around an hour before bed is a good late snack).
- Don't drink water too close to bed (bathroom trips will keep you awake).
- Ensure that you are cool or warm enough (depending on the weather).
- Don't leave the radio or television on while you sleep. If you can't sleep in total silence, opt for a bit of white noise.
- Get enough exercise!

All of the above benefits more than just one aspect of your being. And I know that it's tempting to stay up all night, eating chips and playing games, but your body will thank you if you opt for a book and some apple!

Be Grateful

When we feel down and out, it's easy to forget that we have so much to be grateful for. Even if you may not have things easy, you still have them easier than some other people. I have found that it helps to remind myself that, sure, I might not have a Hollywood mansion, but I have a home and a comfortable bed. That's more than a large number of people on Earth can say.

Once you start making it a priority to be grateful, even for the smallest of things, you will notice a shift in your mentality. Instead of "Oh no, everyone has the newest iPhone and I still have an old iPhone," say, "Everyone has the new iPhone and I'd like to have it, but I'm really lucky to have a smartphone that can do pretty much the same thing."

Even things like running water are things we need to be thankful for. In some countries, people need to walk miles upon miles with buckets for water, and we simply turn a tap. You need to learn to have a mindset that is more focused on what you have than what you don't have.

That brings us to our next point, which is setting goals for yourself. Yes, we need to focus on what we do have, be grateful, and make the most of it. But we still need to set reasonable goals for ourselves. Being content with what you have doesn't mean not striving for more.

It's okay to want to have a big and beautiful home and a successful career one day, as long as you don't obsess over what you don't have right now. You can still work hard for that future dream. Or, taking the iPhone example again, you can find a part-time job and set up a "savings" goal for yourself in order to be able to afford the phone all on your own!

Setting goals for ourselves, not only big ones but very small ones too, helps us to feel accomplished and in control (I mean, as much in control as we can be).

Another great form of self-care is spending time in nature. Sure, the physical aspect is great because you'll be walking, but it's relaxing to stroll lazily through some gardens, for example. In reality, any form of relaxation is good for you. Lowering stress and anxiety is important, and performing relaxing activities will help you do just that. You can meditate, read, sit in a pool, and stare up at the sky (wear sunscreen; you'll thank me when you're over 25) and more. Different things will be considered relaxing for different people, so don't feel like you're limited to what the majority of society deems as relaxing. For example, they'll have you believe that gardening is relaxing; well, if you're anything like me, then gardening will probably just feel like sweaty manual labor to you. But hey, you might actually end up liking it, so don't condemn it if you have not tried it yet.

Your mental health, as mentioned, is important. And it's important to ensure that you take the time to process and validate your feelings. You matter, and how you feel matters. Your mental health can make or break you and your future. And that's not saying that your future is bleak if you might have some mental health issues, not at all. It's saying that your mental health will influence your hygiene, your eating habits, your exercise routine, your grades, friendships, everything.

Your self-care habits will carry you throughout your life and every difficult obstacle that you might run into. No matter how mean the world gets or how dark the tunnel feels, one thing that should never change is your love for yourself.

While on the topic of good habits, I would like to take this time to introduce my newest project that will be coming soon. Your habits are important, and they'll shape much of your quality of life.

We'll delve deeper into that with my next book that will be coming soon, *Make Your Bed First: Become the*

Best Version of Yourself Right Now With a Power That Everyone Has Within Them, But Few People Actually Harness. The Power of Habits.

And don't be too worried if you might have realized that your habits could use a little work because the great thing about habits is that they can be learned. Just because you've picked up a few bad habits in your life doesn't mean that they have to stick. You can unlearn them and replace them with good habits. It's a whole new journey that I invite you to join me on. Being self-confident, together with having positive habits, will truly help you succeed throughout your life and ensure that you have the tools to make it to adulthood and not only survive but "thrive," as they say.

This chapter focused on different things that you need to take care of yourself and why self-care is important. I need you to remember that none of this will happen overnight, and you might find it difficult to find the motivation to actually get all these little self-care practices done. Once you get into the groove, though, you'll see that the benefits will help you to stay in the right direction, and hey, you'll form some positive habits along the way.

In our next chapter, we will discuss mindfulness techniques to help you stay present, reduce stress, and develop a positive body image. We're going to accept what we cannot change, learn to love it, and make the best of it!

4

MINDFUL SELF-ACCEPTANCE

To accept ourselves as we are means to value our imperfections as much as our perfections.

— SANDRA BIERIG

In this modern era, you've likely heard about mindfulness at some point, but do you really know the meaning of the term?

According to the American Psychological Association (2022), mindfulness refers to being aware of one's inner state and the environment. By practicing mindfulness, people can break free of harmful or habitual patterns of behavior by simply observing their thoughts, emotions, and other present experiences without judgment or immediate reaction.

You see, none of us are flawless, and that's perfectly okay. We all make mistakes, have insecurities, and sometimes feel like we don't measure up.

Mindful self-acceptance begins with a simple yet powerful realization—you are not defined by your past, your insecurities, or what others think of you. You are unique, and that's amazing.

Mindfulness is a big part of this journey. It's about being present here and now instead of worrying about the future or dwelling on the past. Practicing mindfulness teaches you to observe your thoughts without judging yourself. You start embracing your emotions as messengers of your inner world. You begin to see your experiences as valuable lessons that have shaped you. You should treat yourself with the same kindness and understanding that you would offer to your best friend.

Imagine for a moment that you could silence that voice inside you, the voice that says you're not good enough or that you don't deserve love and acceptance. Self-compassion is the understanding that in your vulnerability, you find strength, and in your mistakes, you find opportunities to grow.

Here's the secret to mindful self-acceptance: It sets you free to be your authentic self. You don't have to pretend to be someone you're not, and you don't have to hide your quirks and flaws. Embracing who you are, with all your imperfections, is where true freedom begins.

MINDFULNESS TECHNIQUES

Now that you have a rough idea of what mindfulness actually is, you start trying some mindfulness techniques. What we're going to focus on here is the reduction of stress, staying present, accepting ourselves, and looking at making our body image more positive.

Contrary to popular belief, mindfulness is not only meditation and mantras, although those can be super helpful, and we'll likely talk about them as well. Mindfulness can be as simple as focusing on your breathing and the sounds around you to kind of "ground" yourself.

Anxiety and Stress

Let's begin with techniques for reducing anxiety. Don't think that just because you're not experiencing major panic attacks, you are not experiencing anxiety. It comes in many shapes and sizes, and it does not discriminate. Stress often goes hand in hand with anxiety, and at your age, I absolutely understand why. There is so much pressure on teens today to perform academically, to look and act perfect, to conform to what society deems as "normal," and more. All that pressure mixed together is the perfect recipe for stress and anxiety.

Firstly, know that doing your best is good enough. You don't have to always be top of your class or be the best at everything. As long as you know that you've put your all into it, that's good enough. I know that you might have heard that as well, but I also know that it doesn't always sink in as it should.

I want you to take a moment to look in the mirror and tell yourself that you are enough and your best is good enough. Don't just do it once because some stranger in a book told you to do it regularly. Whenever you feel that the pressure gets too much, take a breath and remind yourself that you're giving your best and that it's good enough.

Stress and anxiety can actually negatively impact your physical self just as much as your mental self. The most common negative effects of stress and anxiety are elevated pulse, digestive issues, trouble sleeping, headaches, and even elevated blood pressure (Cherney, 2020). Take it from me: Your blood pressure is something you need to take seriously from a young age, as a side note.

Here is a list of activities that you can try:

- Take a walk, and switch off from the internet. Focus on your thoughts, and don't punish yourself if your thoughts wander off to negativity. As they often say in meditation sessions, "gently bring your thoughts back to where you want them to be."
- Yes, you can actually try meditation. Meditation isn't complicated; you can simply sit in a comfortable space and follow a meditation from your phone. YouTube has great guided meditations, but if you want help with more than just meditation, I would definitely recommend the "Calm" app. This app has daily meditations and much more.
- Focus on the good and not just the bad of a situation. So, you're anxious because you've

had a fight with a loved one; yes, it isn't pleasant. But an argument means that you've both voiced what bothers you, and that gives you an opportunity to work on the relationship and make each other happier.
- Make time for art, any kind of art. You don't have to be a modern Picasso to get "artsy," and remember that there are different forms of art. Art therapy has been used for generations, and there's a reason why they have art therapy in places like mental health hospitals: it works.
- Progressive muscle relaxation is when you tense certain muscles and then relax them (Capecchi, 2022). You can start with your face, then your shoulders, and move down throughout the rest of your body until the very tip of your toes. Once you've completed the cycle, you should feel more relaxed. And you can do it as many times as necessary.

Stay Present

It's easy to dwell on thoughts of what you still need to do, the project that you're behind on, or what you're wearing for that school function, but you need to be able to stay in the moment and actually enjoy life! Whatever you're stressing about will likely not get worse if you take a moment to enjoy a meal with your family or have a swim with friends.

One of the most famous techniques for bringing yourself back to the moment and possibly for fighting a panic attack as well is the 5-step grounding technique. This technique has been used for years and has been mentioned by many experts.

You'll begin by finding 5 things that you can see, 4 things you can touch, 3 things you can hear, 2 you can smell, and one you can taste.

By focusing your senses on things presently around you, you can bring your mind back from where it was wandering.

It was not long ago that the daughter of a close friend went through a difficult time. For the sake of privacy, her real name will not be used. We'll call her "Sarah."

Sarah had lost both her grandparents on the same day, and it put a massive strain on her family. At the same time, she had mock exams coming up, and she was extremely self-conscious about her appearance.

She started isolating herself because she couldn't pull her head out of the dark hole that it had fallen into. And even when she was around us, she was very much like an ostrich with its head in a hole because she wasn't really present. Whenever her mind wandered into negativity, she would begin biting her nails.

It became such a bad habit (in the span of three weeks) that her fingers bled.

It was on a Friday evening when I finally thought it was time to speak up. Of course, I spoke to her parents first.

And we arranged a dinner at their house so that she didn't need to be forced to go anywhere. It began normally and she said hello, but quickly retreated to her room once more. Once we began serving appetizers, I went to her room and asked her to join us. She was hesitant, but I believe she didn't want to be rude, and so she followed me.

Within the first ten minutes, her head lowered, and she began biting the nail of her left thumb.

This was my shot, I thought. Now, I needed to be careful because she was in a delicate state already, but I gently touched my hand to hers to lower it down. I nodded at her parents and they nodded in return, continuing their chat as though they were oblivious to us. See, I didn't want her to feel self-conscious by bringing everyone's attention to her.

I explained the 5-step grounding technique to her, and we did it together. After the first time, she was visibly more relaxed, so I suggested we try again.

It was when I nodded to her mother again that they began including us in their conversation again. I could see Sarah taking part with interest, and when she withdrew into herself again half an hour later, I watched her close her eyes and perform the action again (I assumed). When the end of the evening came, she thanked me, and according to her parents, she has been doing much better.

It's not to say that this is not a cure-all, far from it. But it will help you, and the more you try, the easier it will become until you feel confident enough to simply mindfully recognize that your mind has wandered too far, and you can gently bring it back.

When you stay in the present, you enhance your quality of life. Let the world burn for a couple of hours. Enjoy it while you can!

Mindfulness and Your Body

By being mindful and kind to yourself, you can learn to accept who you are and your body. Some things can't be changed, and if you can learn to embrace those parts of yourself and accept them, you might just be going in the right direction.

When you're mindful, you can become more aware of yourself. This helps you recognize the good, the bad, and the unchangeable. Not to mention self-reflection. When you can reflect on your thoughts and behaviors, you can recognize what might be damaging your self-esteem.

Your body is the only body you have unless we somehow have some kind of technological advance that can give us some robotic body in the near future; doubtful though. Spending your entire life hating your body sounds pretty awful to me.

You need to learn to love yourself by looking at the good things your body can do. Scientifically, the human body is incredibly impressive. But beyond science, you are blessed to have each ability that you have. Even if you might not have all the abilities of others, the ones you do have are precious.

Research shows that accepting yourself without judgment plays an important role in your self-esteem (LPC, 2014).

What We Don't Like Talking About

Eating disorders are a topic that society isn't always comfortable talking about, and of course, in the cases where it is, it can often be romanticized by Hollywood movies.

I know a young woman who has struggled with bulimia nervosa (binge and purge) for over ten years and it had a massive impact on almost every aspect of her life. It was through mindfulness and acceptance that she finally began to heal.

You see, being mindful of your body and its needs is important. Your body needs food as fuel and it needs enough liquids to survive. It's okay to give it what it needs and to indulge in a little treat every now and again.

Actively making a point of listening to your body is just as mindful as listening to your thoughts.

And before we continue, no, not only women have trouble with eating disorders. All too often, men are left at the short end of the stick, but they suffer just as much as women do.

What you can do to practice listening to your body is as simple as taking a seat as though you were about to meditate and feel your body. Instead of watching your thoughts without judgment, listen to whether your body is telling you that it needs food, water, rest, or whatever else it may need.

They say that eating slowly and savoring each bite helps with mindful eating. I can imagine that this would be the case because when you eat slowly and without too many distractions around you, you can more easily listen to your body when it says that it has had enough or that it needs more.

In this chapter, we covered mindfulness and self-acceptance. In the next chapter, we'll talk about building healthy relationships and why that is important.

5

BUILDING HEALTHY RELATIONSHIPS

I used to think the worst thing in life was to end up all alone, it's not. The worst thing in life is to end up with people that make you feel all alone.

— ROBIN WILLIAMS

Being surrounded by people doesn't necessarily mean that you're going to be happy or feel fulfilled. It's the people that you have a true connection with that mean the most. But it's not always just as simple as that. Some relationships may mean the world to you, but they might not exactly be positive, fruitful, or generally "good" for you. Let's explore what that means and how we can build healthy relationships.

WHAT IS A HEALTHY RELATIONSHIP AND WHAT IS NOT?

Healthy relationships are all about communication, boundaries, empathy, and respect. You should be able to freely express yourself without fear of judgment. You try your best to listen to each other and try to understand where the other person is coming from.

Trust is the number one foundation of any healthy relationship. You need to learn to trust and be trusted, which builds emotional security and intimacy. Keeping promises, being reliable, and respecting each other's privacy are all part of the trust game.

Another important layer of the foundation is respect. You need to treat each other with kindness, consideration, and appreciation. Valuing each other's opinions and boundaries is a big part of that. There is no room for belittling, mocking, or coercing each other. It's all about equality and lifting each other up.

Independence is super important, too. Personal growth and independence should be a part of your relationships. You can and should support each other's goals, interests, and friendships while still maintaining your own identity.

Conflict happens, too, but in healthy relationships, you tackle it head-on. Resolve disagreements through compromise, empathy, and problem-solving. No aggression or avoiding the issue should be tolerated. If you keep your feelings to yourself, they will be bottled up, and this may lead to further escalation and frustration. That means that whatever the problem is may not be resolved and, in fact, may become harmful when it wasn't meant to be.

To sum it up, effective communication, trust, respect, independence, equality, and conflict resolution are important for healthy relationships (youth.-gov, n.d.).

The above is very much based on very personal relationships, but it is important to remember that other relationships, such as those with teachers or mentors, are just as important, and their influence can be crucial in your life, even if your relationship isn't an actual friendship.

On the flip side, unhealthy relationships often lack effective communication. Jealousy and control are major red flags. Unhealthy relationships may involve possessiveness, attempts to restrict activities or friendships, and controlling behaviors as well. This goes without saying, but not only romantic relationships are necessarily unhealthy or can include things such as possessiveness. Disrespect is never okay, and name-calling, insults, and belittlement have no place in a healthy relationship.

Manipulation is something that is often found in unhealthy relationships, and it's not something that you should stand for. Guilt-tripping, emotional blackmail, and the silent treatment are all harmful behaviors that should also never be tolerated.

And let's not forget the most serious issue: abuse. Physical, emotional, or verbal abuse is never acceptable and should be addressed immediately. Don't ever think that it can't or won't happen to you. It can, and you need to understand that abuse of any kind is unacceptable.

Why are healthy relationships so important? Well, they teach you crucial life skills like effective communication, emotional intelligence, conflict resolution, setting boundaries, and self-esteem. They also promote respect for diversity and provide emotional support during the rollercoaster teenage years.

On the flip side, unhealthy relationships can seriously harm your mental, emotional, and physical well-being. That's why it's crucial to recognize the signs and seek help from trusted adults, friends, or counselors when needed. It's often the case that people you have healthy relationships with and that you trust can be beneficial for pointing out unhealthy relationships and dealing with them.

The best way that I can think of to explain what unhealthy and healthy relationships look like is by using anecdotes and examples. Therefore, we're going to look at a few scenarios that portray real-life examples of healthy and unhealthy relationships or, rather, behaviors. The behavior of people in certain situations can tell you a lot about what the relationship is generally like.

Example One: Unhealthy

Jenny has been friends with Margie since they were seven years old. They lived next to each other, so it was easy to build a friendship. It was innocent, like most childhood friendships are, and they played together well.

The girls did not attend the same school, but that didn't matter. By the time they had turned thirteen years old, they were best friends. Practically attached by the hip. And this is when the trouble began.

Margie began suggesting that they cut school to hang out together, but that's not so bad, right? Everyone does it now and again (you really shouldn't; you'll regret it when you're older, though).

Jenny was a straight-B student, and she participated in different extracurricular activities as well. Margie wasn't very bothered by school. Her parents were wealthy, and she might have been under the impression that studying wasn't that important. Of course, this isn't to say that this is always the case, but in this situation, it was.

The real problems began when Margie introduced Jenny to her friends, and they were generally not a good influence. This might normally not be a problem because Jenny was a sensible girl who knew right from wrong. Unfortunately, Margie became manipulative and said things like, "You're not a real friend; otherwise, you'd do this with me."

Manipulation can come in many forms, and it's not always as straightforward as that, and that's why we need to be careful. You might think that you'd be clever enough to avoid it, but it hits differently when it comes from someone you really care about.

In this scenario, the relationship became toxic because Margie was manipulating Jenny, and she was also encouraging her to do the wrong things. In the perfect world, Margie would never have gotten involved in any of it, and Jenny might have even been a good influence on her. But this is not the perfect world, and just because you're a good person doesn't mean that you can save everyone.

It's true that if we care for someone, we need to try and help them, but there comes a point where it is crucial for your own physical and mental health to draw the line. It might sound selfish, but you need to put yourself first. I know that you don't want to hear it, but friends come and go. But your mind and your body, as you should know by now, will stick with you until the end.

Example Two: Unhealthy

This scenario is simple: a young boy grew up under difficult circumstances yet worked hard to move away from it. Although he wasn't at the top of his class, he performed well. His weak point was, unfortunately, Math (I can relate). And you wouldn't think it, but the negative influence here was actually his teacher.

This is a true story, by the way.

The teacher constantly belittled the boy and told him that he would never amount to anything because he wasn't good at Math.

It's as simple as that. That is an unhealthy teacher-student relationship. Instead of encouraging him and spending time to help him, he belittled him. In the perfect world, all teachers would be role models that change the lives of their students, and while many absolutely are, you guessed it, this is not the perfect world.

You might be wondering what you can actually do in such a case; a teacher is an authority figure, after all. So, in cases such as this, students may feel powerless. But you're not.

If you're ever in a situation where an authority figure is an unhealthy influence, you need to speak out to an adult you trust. For example, in this case, if I were him, I would visit the principal and have a serious talk.

Do remember, though, that there is a difference between enforcing discipline and being an unhealthy influence. Discipline is a crucial aspect of life, and you'll need to learn to submit to authority; otherwise, you'll definitely have difficulties ahead of you.

Example Three: Unhealthy

This is very common, and it can go both ways. Contrary to popular belief, it's not always boys who pressure their partners into sex. Girls can be the ones who pressure their partners as well.

Let's not use names in this one to avoid selecting a specific gender. But picture a couple who has been dating for a few months or even years (there is no time limit, and being together for a long time does not mean you have to say yes). The one person pressuring the other into sex is wrong and toxic. And it is, once again, not always as straightforward as "if you love me, you'll do it."

Some people can be very subtle, so subtle that you might not even realize it before it goes too far. Be vigilant, and don't let anyone pressure you into doing anything that you do not want to.

Example Four: Unhealthy

Outside of pressure and manipulation, another serious red flag that might sound similar is wanting to "control" you. This doesn't refer to parents or teachers giving you tasks or instructions. This refers to friends and romantic interests wanting to dictate who you spend time with, what you do, what you wear, what music you listen to, or anything else.

If it's not your opinion or in your best interest, nobody should be telling you what to do or what to like. You need to be true to yourself, and you need to give yourself the freedom to explore different aspects of life (safely and responsibly) without being pushed into a certain kind of box by someone in your life.

Again, don't get me wrong, your parents and other trusted adults give you direction because they've likely been where you are and understand certain situations better than we do. I know it's annoying. But hey, why bump your head when you can follow their advice instead?

Example Five: Healthy

Martin and John met a few months ago at a sporting event. They're from different schools, but they hit it off pretty quickly. John felt discouraged because he came in last in a big race, and he had been preparing for a few weeks.

Martin had been visiting and knew that John was thinking of giving up. Perhaps he wasn't good at sports? But Martin didn't have any of it. Instead, he encouraged his new friend and began training with him, even though he, himself, came in second in this race.

In this scenario, sports were the main focus, but the idea behind it is simple and applicable to many different aspects of friendship. What we can do for our friends is encourage and support them. This could easily have gone the wrong way had Martin been one to gloat about his own victory instead of acknowledging his friend's feelings.

Example Six: Healthy

Keeping in line with acknowledging feelings that are an important part of relationships of any kind—whether with family, friends, or romantic partners. I know we don't and won't always understand the feelings of the people in our lives. And some people are not as open to sharing as others are. But the very least we can do is be observant and acknowledge that they might be feeling sad, mad, or frustrated, even if we don't understand why. It's a good idea to try and understand, of course, and to have them talk to us about it.

Example Seven: Healthy

Your sibling has a massive fear of frogs. You kind of think it's silly. I mean, frogs can be kind of cute or gross, depending on who you ask—but being so afraid of them that you want to pass out at the sight of one? Come on.

A friend of yours suggests a prank for your sibling's birthday: fake frogs in the tub. You know, the kind, those slimy, jelly-like ones. It would be a funny prank. You'd probably enjoy your sibling's reaction.

However, you don't agree to it because you respect your sibling enough not to cross such a line. Even if you don't understand why they are so afraid, and you think it's silly, you still respect how they feel about it.

Example Eight: Healthy

Your friend is from a Jewish family and they take their faith seriously. You are not Jewish, but you still respect their special days and traditions. Respecting the beliefs of others is crucial in any healthy relationship, no matter how differently we may feel about certain things.

Example Nine: Healthy

You have trouble opening up about your feelings, but one specific teacher has a certain natural way of helping you feel comfortable. You get to share your feelings with them whenever you need to, and they listen and offer advice as needed.

Example Ten: Healthy

Lizzie and Max have an argument over who is going to be the team lead in the upcoming prom committee. Naturally, they both feel that they are fit for the position. Their friendship could easily have gone sour over the fact, but instead, they agreed to put it to a vote to accept the outcome and support each other.

Example Eleven: Healthy

Your sibling has this annoying habit of whistling all day, every day. It's insane. You don't understand how they even have that much lung capacity.

Instead of bottling it up or yelling at them every time they do it, you sit them down and talk to them about how you feel. Because you approached the situation calmly and gently, they are understanding and they promise to try to do it less often. Of course, since it is a habit, you understand that there won't be absolute silence at first. It will take time to break the habit.

The point is that these simple examples give a massive glimpse into the nature of these relationships and whether they positively influence the people involved or not. Did any of them feel relatable?

EXERCISES

I want you to find a comfortable spot to sit where you may be able to have some privacy for a bit. Take a pen and some paper, and write down the names of the significant people in your life.

This is a serious activity, and you need to really think about how each of them influences you. What do you think can be changed or done to better things that may not be as positive as they can be?

It's important to remember that while certain actions can help us to see the nature of a relationship, it might not always be as easy to cut people out who might not be that good for you.

Ideally, we would want to have only positive relationships and influences in our lives. But that won't always be possible. So, what can you do?

It's okay to try and "fix" a relationship that is significant to you by practicing effective communication and by explaining how you feel. Turning it into a healthy relationship could be possible with dedication and hard work. But do try to remember that there is, once again, a line that you need to draw. If the other person is not receptive to your feelings or suggestions, there is only so much you can do.

In cases where the negative influence may be someone who is, unfortunately, a part of your daily life, it is okay to distance yourself from them. Be sure to remain polite and respectful, but you don't need to get closer to them than necessary. You don't need to share your ins and outs with them.

Look, it's a difficult conversation to have; we don't always want to let go of what may be considered as "bad" for us. But you need to put your well-being first.

What I want you to do next is to sit yourself down and have a stern talk to yourself about your self-worth and what boundaries or values you have. And write these down. Once you have identified your values and boundaries, you need to clearly communicate them with the people in your life, and remember that respect goes both ways. If you want them to respect yours, you need to respect theirs.

The Gist of It

You may not think it now, and I don't know what your situation may be. But you are worthy of respect, love, appreciation, and all those other positive things. Don't let people drag you down or treat you like you don't matter. You matter.

This chapter focused on healthy and unhealthy relationships. The people around you have a massive impact on you, and ensuring that the impact is a positive one is a substantially important task.

In the next chapter, we will be exploring creative outlets, self-expression, and how pursuing passions can boost self-esteem. This one is going to be fun!

6

SELF-EXPRESSION AND CONFIDENCE

A diamond doesn't start out polished and shining. It once was nothing special, but with enough pressure and time, becomes spectacular. I'm that diamond.

— SOLANGE NICOLE

Let's talk about confidence and how it should come from within. Sure, it feels great to hear compliments and praise from others, but what truly matters is how you see yourself. After all, you're the one who will be with yourself for the rest of your life, while others may come and go. Your opinion is the most important one!

Now, how can we boost our confidence and express ourselves without relying on outside validation? Well, here's the secret: Impress yourself! Focus on your passions, creativity, and anything else that truly matters to you. Set goals and put effort into what you love. That's where the magic begins.

But what if your way of expressing yourself doesn't align with the expectations of those around you? Forget about them! You need to be confident enough to be true to yourself and pursue what brings you joy. As long as it's safe and doesn't harm anyone, go for it!

Creative outlets are incredibly important. They can take many forms, from how you dress to art or even playing sports. The possibilities are endless! Let's explore and find what resonates with you.

So, remember, your confidence should come from within. Impress yourself, embrace your unique expression, and pursue what makes you happy. Don't worry about others' opinions.

Let's explore!

CREATIVE OUTLETS

It's no secret that being able to have a creative outlet is beneficial. There are actually instances where people who may struggle to communicate use creative ways to express themselves. That's not the only way in which creative outlets are beneficial, though.

Since the literal beginning of time, self-expression has been the heartbeat of our existence. From the moment we could communicate, we always looked for ways to share our thoughts, emotions, and experiences. This desire for self-expression is related to our quest for self-esteem and confidence.

Self-expression is the process of revealing our innermost thoughts, feelings, and unique perspectives to the world. It's kind of like the art of being ourselves, unapologetically and authentically.

Self-expression comes in many forms, from writing to visual arts and the rhythmic beats of music or even food! It is through these creative avenues that we can paint a picture of what the inside of our minds looks like.

Creativity is the key that unlocks the door to self-expression. It encompasses a vast range of activities that allow us to channel our thoughts, emotions, and experiences into actual things. Consider the artist who uses a canvas to translate their emotions into colors and shapes or the musician who composes melodies that resonate with their deepest feelings. These acts of creation are like mirrors reflecting our inner landscapes.

Creative outlets are super therapeutic, too. Not to get too technical, but when we're creative, our brains actually release special chemicals that help us feel happy (Martino, 2021). Not to mention the feeling of accomplishment and satisfaction you feel when you've done something creative or taken part in an activity that you would describe as your outlet.

Our passions are the fuel that the "cars" of our lives use. When we immerse ourselves in our interests and passions, we form a better connection with ourselves. This connection is the actual foundation of self-esteem.

When in Doubt, Let it out!

Life can hit like a sack of rocks, and it may be related to school, social life, your self-esteem, or more, but we all have our "down" times. I say, let your feelings be the canvas of your creation.

Creative expression is a powerful tool for processing and coping with life's challenges. When adversity strikes, be it personal loss, stress, or uncertainty, creative endeavors provide a safe space to channel our emotions.

Think about some of the most famous songs you know throughout history; most of them are based on heartbreak, unfortunately. Some are about love, too, though. And that further explains the power of using emotion to further your creativity. These lyrics, or compositions, were woven together in a different state of mind, making them unique.

That's not to say you need to be sad in order to create something worth anything, but using your emotions and transferring them into your work is the number one secret here.

How We Inspire Others

Our creative expressions are not limited to personal gain; they have the power to inspire and connect us with others, too, you know. When we share our creations, we invite others into our world.

We can inspire other people to express themselves more fully and to be themselves unapologetically. Think of it like a revolution: If you can be your true self and show your unique character to the world, sharing your creative outlet with them, you might just inspire them to do the same.

An unfortunate truth is that many young people suffer immensely because they cannot be themselves for whatever reason and in whatever context. This leads to depression, suicidal thoughts, and more. But if we can encourage true self-acceptance, we might not only make a more gentle world, we might save lives.

The journey of self-expression through creative outlets is a profound voyage of self-discovery, healing, and empowerment. When we engage in these pursuits, we not only communicate our innermost thoughts and emotions but also nurture our self-esteem and confidence.

Who Can Have A Creative Outlet?

The fantastic news is that anyone, yes, including you, can have a creative outlet. Creativity isn't reserved for the chosen few; it's something that is buried inside all of us, and it simply needs to be watered in order to blossom. AKA, put some time into it! It doesn't matter if you're an aspiring artist, a budding musician, a passionate writer, or if you have a unique talent waiting to be discovered. Creativity is a universal language, and you are part of this creative world.

What do you need?

The short answer?

Curiosity, passion, courage, time, patience, support, and mindfulness, according to John Graham-Pole (2000) in his book *Illness and the Art of Creative Self-Expression: Stories and Exercises from the Arts for Those With Chronic Illness.*

Hobbies

The main difference lies in the focus and purpose of the activity. Hobbies are typically for fun and relaxation, encompassing a wide array of interests, while creative outlets are specifically centered around artistic or creative expression. Some activities can overlap, as a hobby may also be a creative outlet if it involves artistic expression.

Hobbies are more than just fun, though; they hold a special place in our lives. Whether it's painting, playing an instrument, gardening, cooking, or even stargazing, hobbies have the power to bring us joy and boost our self-esteem.

Hobbies allow us to escape the daily grind and unwind while doing something we like, much like with a creative outlet. When we engage in our hobbies, time flies by, and we enter a state of "flow" where everything else fades away, and we're fully present in the moment. This is super helpful for the whole mindfulness thing.

The benefits of hobbies go beyond just having fun. They can reduce stress and provide a mental escape from worries and anxieties, again similar to creative outlets.

Some hobbies (especially the ones overlapping with creative outlets) also offer a fantastic opportunity for skill development. As we spend time honing our craft, we naturally become better at it. The sense of progress and mastery that comes with improving is really satisfying.

The thing about hobbies is that they can also help with your social life. In a way, I suppose sports can be classified as a hobby, but in a special way, I still believe that they count as creative outlets for others.

Having hobbies helps us define who we are and contributes to our sense of identity and individuality. Engaging in activities we love reinforces the idea that our interests matter and that we are unique individuals with something valuable to offer. When we're happy and content, we naturally feel better about ourselves, and hobbies typically trigger those feelings. This positive emotional state spills over into other aspects of our lives, further elevating our self-esteem. Hobbies teach us perseverance and resilience.

What About Celebrities?

Okay, so everyone loves celebrities, even if you love completely different ones. And the one thing they all have in common (most of them anyway)? They have interesting hobbies or creative outlets.

You see, celebrities, as mentioned before, are just like us. And they have flaws and insecurities and all the other bad things, just like us. But they also have the positive aspects of humanity!

For many celebrities, their careers began as hobbies or creative outlets, but unfortunately, once it becomes work, it rarely remains relaxing and rarely retains all the original benefits.

One of the most interesting hobbies, and probably one of the scarier ones I have read about, is Oprah Winfrey's beekeeping hobby (Nawab, 2023). Yup, picture the original live TV star in the full sci-fi-looking get-up. Not a care in the world about who sees her or thinks what. But then again, I suppose that if I had a net worth as high as she did, I would probably also not care what others think (I kid).

Also, have you ever heard of the game *Tomb Raider*? Well, they have live-action movies, and Angeline Jolie is the star of the show. Guess what? She is actually pretty close to as adventurous as her on-screen character. She is a licensed pilot and is really passionate about knife throwing (Abi-Khalil, 2023). Who would have thought?

Just like the two above, many other celebs have many different hobbies or creative outlets. I mean, think about Meryl Streep and her knitting, like, lady, I would wear whatever you knit forever.

Don't Let Yourself Be Judged

It can often happen that people want to judge us for the things that we enjoy or are passionate about. Take Miss Jolie above, a woman throwing knives and flying planes? Gah!

That's the mentality of many people, unfortunately. Think about Snoop Dog baking and cooking; many people frown upon it because of traditional stereotypes and for many other reasons.

One of the important lessons that you will ever learn is to accept yourself for who you are and to let go of the opinions of others. So, you enjoy finger painting, so what if other "artists" call you a "toddler." It's creative, and if you enjoy it, go for it.

I don't try to be someone I'm not. I try to be myself, and I think that's the most important thing.

— ZENDAYA

Let these words remain with you, and not only because Zendaya is a successful celebrity, but because it's true.

In order to be able to express ourselves in the way that we deserve to, we need to be confident enough to do so. And in order to grow and further develop our confidence, we need to allow ourselves to flourish. It's a cycle of positivity.

The truth is, there will probably always be someone who judges you for something, no matter who or what it is. The best thing that you can do is to let it run off of you like water off a duck's back.

It doesn't matter whether our passions are as innocent as knitting (too old school) or as interesting as knife throwing (too rough); someone is going to have something to say about it.

You do you, and don't let the negativity of this floating rock in space get you down. You're a literal vessel of one of the most complex structures in the universe, the human body and brain. That alone can be your confidence boost for the day.

In this chapter, we discussed creative outlets, hobbies, and why/how they're good for you. In the next chapter, we'll delve deeper into peer pressure and how social media plays a role. This is going to be a deep one!

7

PEER PRESSURE AND HOW SOCIAL MEDIA PLAYS A ROLE

Why fit in, when you were born to stand out?

— DR SEUSS

In a world that values appearances and constantly bombards us with images of what they would describe as the "perfect" bodies for both boys and girls, peer pressure plays a significant role in shaping our perceptions of body image.

I totally understand that teens often find themselves susceptible to societal expectations and the opinions of others. It's hard to think a certain way when everyone is pushing you in a different direction. But it's not impossible to break away from it.

Social media also plays a big role, once again here not only for the reasons we've explored before but also because of the way that peer pressure is taken away from only being in public settings to your personal space. With social media, it's like the pressure from other people never ends. It follows you from the moment you open your eyes to the moment you close them.

In the past, teens were pressured when they were around other people, but now, communication is way easier. Yes, it's great to be able to communicate with each other frequently, but it can also be damaging.

THE POWER IT WIELDS

Peer pressure can have a massive effect on how you see your body. It doesn't matter whether the pressure is direct or indirect. The standards that are set out by the media and the people around us, as you know by now, can be unrealistic, to say the least. It's easy to want to fall in line with these standards and to want to "go with the flow." But let me tell you, it's much more rewarding in the long run to "swim upstream."

The immense desire to fit in and to look like the "perfect" pictures that are painted by everyone around us can easily lead to super unhealthy attitudes toward our body image. I know that it can feel like it's easier to just avoid the criticism that will undoubtedly be thrown at us.

I might not be a teenager anymore, but I was. And I am a parent, too. And while technology and everything changes, some things do stay the same. For example, the pressure to look certain ways; let's and act certain ways will probably always be there.

It's not just about how you look and your body; let's talk about your actions as well.

How Your Actions Influence Your Self-Esteem

Not everyone understands that the things you do and take part in actually also influence your self-esteem, body image, and more. You might be wondering how? Well, it's a simple concept.

Picture this: there's some random TikTok challenge that has teens licking toilet bowls (yes, this actually happened, don't do it), and everyone is doing it. So, you feel pressured to do it as well, and eventually, you do. You will likely feel disgusted and disappointed in yourself for kind of stooping to such a level. This can also be dangerous because the chance that you'll get sick is absolutely high.

Now, this gets even more dangerous when it comes to things such as illicit drugs and alcohol. When you're young, you don't always realize the negative effects that these things can have on both your mind and body. Not to mention your self-worth.

As a human being, you have your own unique set of values and beliefs. Regardless of what they are, going against them can make us feel guilty and can dampen our self-esteem.

Sometimes, accepting yourself for who you are means accepting your values, too. And in a world where those are often not taken seriously, that can be a difficult task.

> *The most important thing in your life is to live your life with integrity and to not give in to peer pressure to try to be something that you're not.*
>
> — ELLEN DEGENERES

If you're not comfortable with something, don't let the pressure of others bully you into doing it. It doesn't matter if your beliefs are wildly different from those around you; you are worthy of respect, and respect starts by respecting yourself. If you have no respect for yourself, it will be difficult for others to respect you. This is because people often follow our lead.

This can be used to our advantage or disadvantage. For example, let's say you're self-conscious about your nose, and you begin teasing yourself so that you can say that you laugh with others instead of them laughing at you. Firstly, it's silly to ever talk down on yourself for anything, and if you've ever done anything like this, then you know very well that even though you may be laughing, you still feel hurt. This can easily lead to others thinking that it's okay to tease you for it since you're okay with it.

Similarly, if you stand up for yourself and for who you are, it could trigger a more positive outcome by leading others to treat you the same way.

The old saying goes that we should treat others as we wish to be treated, and while that is absolutely true, we also need to treat ourselves the way we want others to treat us. You don't have to stand and take any "down talking" from anyone, much less yourself.

You need to be your biggest fan and number one cheerleader. Contrary to popular belief, it's not selfish to look out for yourself. I'm not saying that you should disregard the feelings of others, though. All I am saying is that you need to take care of yourself first because, as another old saying goes, "charity begins at home."

There are Negative Effects, But Don't Beat Yourself Up

Allowing your perception of yourself to be altered by peer pressure or allowing yourself to fall and forget your values can have many side effects—more than simply feeling unworthy or guilty.

Peer pressure related to body image can have various negative consequences. The constant pursuit of an "ideal" body can lead to unhealthy behaviors such as excessive dieting, over-exercising, or even developing eating disorders like anorexia or bulimia. These behaviors can take a severe toll on one's physical and mental health.

We've previously discussed some of these disorders, so I believe you should understand by now that it's quite serious.

The constant pursuit of acceptance and validation from others can also lead to various mental health issues and even have a negative effect on your future. When you're so focused on what others think, you might just leave your grades, family, friends, or other important parts of your life behind.

Look, I know that this is an uncomfortable conversation to have, and you might not even want to hear it. But it's crucial for us to discuss these things. If I don't tell you, life might just cruelly show you.

You might be sitting here now, realizing that you might have already been the victim of peer pressure and more. And if that is the case, I need you to take a breath and calm down. It doesn't mean that you've fallen too far to get up; you're never too low to rise above anything.

> *Yeah, I think that I have like, faltered, you know, as a human. My message isn't perfectly defined. I have, as a human being, fallen to peer pressure.*
>
> — KANYE WEST

If someone like Kanye West, a literal celebrity, can admit that he has fallen victim to peer pressure, then you can too. And it's okay to admit our mistakes. It doesn't matter what you may have done in the past; what matters is what you do from here on out.

In the famous old Disney movie that you may or may not be familiar with, *The Lion King*, there is a scene where Rafiki (a kind of wise monkey) tries to make a point by hitting Simba (a lion) over the head with a stick. When the lion asks him what it was for, the monkey replies with, "It doesn't matter; it's in the past."

"But that hurt," Simba replied.

"Ah yes, the past can hurt. But the way I see it, you can either run from it or learn from it."

When he aims to hit the lion again, the lion actually manages to duck and miss being hit. Symbolizing that he has learned from the past, and even though it hurt, it taught him a lesson! This probably feels like a silly story, but the message behind it is clear.

Your past is in the past, but instead of feeling guilty and beating yourself up for it or even trying to run from it, you can learn from it. And when you've learned from it, you can aim to do better in the present and the future.

True Confidence Should Come From Within

Confidence is knowing who you are and not changing it a bit because of someone's version of reality is not your reality.

— SHANNON L. ALDER

Have you ever heard the saying that "what's normal for the spider is chaos for the fly"? Well, that probably applies more to our lives than we think.

For example, to someone raised in a wealthy home, it might be normal to be able to wear all kinds of brand-name clothing. But to someone who was not raised in a wealthy home, it might not be that normal.

That's all perfectly fine, but the problem comes in when we try to make one person's "normal" someone else's. In this particular scenario, the person who may not be as wealthy could easily feel rejected and unworthy if they cannot afford what the other can. And it has happened that some people might even resort to crime. No, no, I am not saying that this always happens. But it has, and that just goes to show how serious the situation actually is. If people are pushing their standards and their "normal" on others so hard that they feel the need to resort to crime, you know something is wrong.

The truth? Having those brand-name clothing items will likely not make you feel very confident for very long. That's because true confidence needs to come from inside ourselves. If you don't love and accept yourself, your confidence won't grow, no matter how many material things you have.

The same can be said for the person who comes from a wealthy family. The things they have won't necessarily help them to love themselves, no matter how "on trend" they are. If they are not content with themselves, material things will mean nothing.

Strategies to Maintain a Healthy Perspective and Beating Peer Pressure

With all of the above in mind, we need to look at some strategies that we can implement in order to help guide us in the right direction. After all, having all the information in the world will do you no good if you don't know how to use it to help you.

The first step is to foster self-acceptance. You need to actually tell yourself that, hey, everyone is different. Diversity is what makes our world so special. People look different, come from different backgrounds, and have different genes. And you know what? That's a good thing! Once you can get it into your head that everyone is different, and that's okay, you are well on your way to self-acceptance.

How can you actually get yourself to "believe" that? For starters, maybe stop looking at celebrities online and stop scrolling social media daily. If you bombard yourself with the world's ideals, you're more likely to want to conform to them. Just look in the mirror and say, yeah, I might not be the tallest guy in class, but not everyone is that tall. That's okay.

It's important to be mindful of your thoughts; don't punish yourself for dwelling on the negative, but rather remind yourself to break away from the negative. And gently focus on more positive thoughts instead. There is no one-size-fits-all definition of beauty. Embrace your individuality and acknowledge that beauty comes in various shapes and sizes.

The next thing you can do is focus on your self-care and remember the importance of taking care of yourself.

While you're focusing on your positive perspective, remember that the best thing you can do is to try and beat peer pressure. The best and number one defense against peer pressure will always be choosing your circle wisely.

While it would be ideal to be confident enough in yourself to be able to let things go and swim upstream, that's harder than it looks. You need to ensure that the people you surround yourself with are people who have similar views, beliefs, and values as you do.

This doesn't mean that you can't be friends with everyone; sure, you can. But your inner circle needs to be like-minded people.

Your closest friends and family are supposed to be your rock of support, and we are not supposed to need to pretend around them or need to fight for our views around them. You know that your friendship is strong and healthy when you can be yourself without constantly needing to fight against some kind of pressure.

It can happen that someone very close to you may be pressuring you into things that make you uncomfortable. This is something we would like to avoid, but if it cannot be avoided then you need to be able to have open and serious conversations about boundaries.

It's okay to set boundaries with friends and family. In fact, it's crucial for many reasons. See, boundaries are not always the big and serious things we think about. They can be small, but that doesn't make them less important. For example, we all have that one family member who likes a kiss on the cheek when they are greeted. Some people don't mind it, but many do. If it is something that you're not comfortable with, you have the right to politely say so and to stand your ground.

It could even just be a hug; if you don't like hugging people, you shouldn't have to. In healthy relationships, people won't force you to.

Boundaries are also regarding your values and beliefs. Say you do have a close person that, for example, might be comfortable with telling lies to get out of trouble or skipping class. It's okay to tell them that while you care for them, you don't feel comfortable with doing this and would appreciate it if they respected your decision. People who care about you and how you feel should accept it when you express your feelings.

Remember, though, it Is a two-way street, and if you expect people to accept and respect your boundaries and feelings, you need to do the same. If your best friend does not like being touched, don't touch them. No matter how much you care about them and would like to hug them every time you see them.

If we can learn to accept each other and respect each other, we will be on our way to a better world.

One, respect and accept ourselves. Two, respect and accept each other.

Further strategies:

- Remember to be grateful for everything you do have and to not dwell on only what you do not have.
- Figure out what is important to you and why. Self-reflection is a crucial part of discovering yourself.
- Let yourself explore things safely. You don't have to be labeled as a "metalhead," or a "popular kid." Let go of labels and don't conform to what people typically expect. You can like ballet and football.
- Set clear goals for yourself, but don't only set goals. Plan around how you will achieve these goals and why they are significant (Drury, 2019).
- Don't lose sleep over other people. Ensure that you get enough rest, and set up a good bedtime routine to get yourself to unwind properly before it's time to sleep so that your mind can focus on the task at hand rather than what happened during the day.

As a part of self-care, sleep is crucial. So remember, no screens at least an hour before bed, no caffeine after 4–5 p.m. (preferably, don't have caffeine at all if possible), and don't drink a full glass of water just before bed (bathroom breaks disturb sleep).

In this chapter, we had a look at peer pressure and how it can negatively affect us, as well as social media and more.

The impact of peer pressure on body image is a complex issue that many individuals face. However, it's crucial to remember that your worth is not determined by your appearance. If we can continue embracing self-acceptance, surrounding ourselves with positive influences, and making informed choices, we can counteract the negative effects of peer pressure and maintain a healthy perspective on body image. It's time to celebrate our uniqueness and encourage others to do the same.

In the next chapter, we'll take a look at when you need to ask for professional help and what you may expect when help comes along.

IT'S OKAY TO ASK FOR HELP

I think the hardest part to get to is that point of asking for help or reaching out to other people and being honest with yourself.

— MARY-KATE OLSEN

No matter how many words of encouragement I give you or you give yourself, sometimes, for some people, it will just not be enough. And you know what? That's okay. Every obstacle in life is different for every person who experiences it. Just because your sibling coped fine with, say, your parent's divorce doesn't mean you have to.

So, how do you know if you need help, how and who do you ask, and what can you expect?

KNOW WHEN TO SPEAK UP

There are different mental health disorders that can make it difficult to cope with even everyday life. And if you're in a situation where you might feel as though there is no light at the end of the tunnel, let me tell you, there is. You don't have to struggle as much as you are struggling. There is so much more to life, and you deserve to experience every bit of it.

If you experience more of the following than not, then it might be time to speak up and ask for help:

- insomnia or excessive sleeping
- constant irritability
- constantly feeling like you're not good enough, or hyper fixating on what you perceive as "flaws"
- thoughts of self-harm, or self-harm
- a constant feeling of doom

- bouts of anxiety or panic attacks that increase your heart rate or have you feel like you can't breathe
- feeling like you might pass out constantly
- feeling generally "down" for no apparent or clear reason
- excessive nightmares
- if you have experienced any trauma that you may struggle to deal with
- trouble with concentrating on school work or in general
- feeling like you would rather isolate yourself more than 50% of the time
- experiencing phases of feeling "high," followed by excessive "low" feelings in a constant loop
- any kind of delusions or hallucinations
- feeling like everyone and everything is out to get you

This is not an exhaustive list and there may or may not be many more things you could add or subtract from the list. Experiencing some of these doesn't mean there is something wrong with you. That is something you need to get out of your head right now. It just means you need a little extra help, and there is nothing wrong with that,

I cannot in good conscience tell you that you definitely have a kind of mental illness. You may, or you may not. But the important thing is that if you experience some of these, it's time to ask for help.

How Do You Ask For Help and Who Do You Ask For Help?

That's the real question, isn't it? With so much unnecessary stigma surrounding anything that may have to do with your mental health, it can be difficult to know exactly how you should ask for help.

Not to mention, you may not have the best relationship with the adults in your life. It can happen that the adults in your life may not understand what you're going through, and there could be an answer to it; if you ask for help, you can find out.

So, the very first thing you need to understand is that open communication is key. You cannot ask for help or receive help, for that matter, if you're not willing to talk about what may be wrong.

Any feelings of shame or guilt need to go "out the windoooow." It's not easy when you feel ashamed or shy, but this is one of those moments in life where you need to bite the bullet, swallow your pride, and speak up. You will look back in a few years from now and thank yourself for standing up for you.

If you're truly not comfortable with standing in front of someone and telling them about your struggles, don't let that get you down, either. It happens and not all of us have the same abilities. It can almost be seen as a form of public speaking and you may feel vulnerable and exposed. And that's okay.

What you can do instead is either record yourself speaking, type up a text message, or even write a letter. You can begin your message by stating that you didn't feel comfortable speaking in person but that this is a serious matter.

Choosing who you're going to speak to may be even more difficult; it needs to be an adult that you trust and can rely on. While it would be ideal if this could be your parent/s, I recognize that not everyone has a comfortable or good relationship with their parents for whatever reason there may be. This should not stop you from asking for help.

A trusted teacher or school counselor is a great alternative, and if you honestly feel like you don't know who to talk to, speak to a friend who can help you speak up for yourself.

Don't forget that even extended family members such as your cousins or uncles and aunts can also help you if you feel comfortable speaking to them.

During my lifetime, I've seen teenagers leave letters under principal's doors and many similar things too. It doesn't matter how you ask for help; what matters is that you do.

You may not really think it's important now, but believe me, it is, and when you're older, you will either be grateful that you got a little bit of extra help and support at a young age, or you'll regret not getting it.

What To Expect

Every experience is different, and what you expect is heavily dependent on what your unique situation may be. However, let's look at some things that you might expect.

Firstly, following your speaking up, you can probably expect the person you asked for help to have a talk about what you're dealing with. Some adults have the same issues that you do, so they may send someone else to speak to you instead. Or they may send someone more qualified.

The important thing here is to remember that honesty is crucial. People can't help you if you're not 100% honest about what you are experiencing and how you feel. Don't be afraid to get into the nitty gritty bits, either.

Next, depending on your unique situation, you may be referred to a professional for a consultation. In some cases, this might be a visit to the school counselor first. The school counselor can likely better refer you to someone who is specifically qualified to help you.

If you are referred to a psychologist for therapy, to a psychiatrist for medication, or to any other outside professional, don't be alarmed. It's easy to feel overwhelmed and afraid, but you need to take a deep breath and remind yourself that this is for your own benefit.

Mental health professionals will know how to help you, regardless of what that might mean for you, specifically. Be open to their suggestions, even if they make you feel a little uncomfortable at first. Remember, a professional will never force you into things that really make you feel uncomfortable, but you still need to put a little effort in as well.

Different professionals will have different settings or office spaces. But it is likely that they will be set up in a way that makes it comfortable for you or as comfortable as possible. Personally, I enjoy a very informal office space. I also have soothing water sounds playing in the background to help people feel relaxed.

If the professional you are speaking to takes notes while you speak, don't be alarmed; this is an important part of their assisting you. We need to take notes and go over them in order to thoroughly assess you.

Lean on Your Support

No matter what happens, who you have to deal with, or where this journey takes you, you need to lean on your support system. It may be a bit of a tough journey ahead of you, and that's not necessarily a bad thing. You need to remember that you're not alone. You have people who care about you.

And even if you may feel utterly alone sometimes, you're not. But if you do find that the people closest to you may just not understand what you're going through or how to support you, then it is important to let them know how best they can support you. Don't just expect everyone to know what to do and how to act. They may be as new to this as you are.

Another important thing to remember is that there are support groups of all kinds out there. Don't be afraid to resort to social media or Google to have a look at what kinds of support groups might be near you. A support group may begin as a group of strangers, but they might just become some of your closest friends in time.

Remember that it is good to surround yourself with people who genuinely care about you. Don't let anyone try to belittle you for anything that you may be going through. This brings me to an important part of your journey: cutting off toxic people.

Previously, we discussed the importance of healthy relationships, and this is no different. If you find yourself going through a hard time and needing support, and someone is reacting insensitively, you don't have to just "take it." Once again, you are worthy of respect and love!

Wherever this takes you, just know that you'll come out on the other side with a better sense of self-worth and many more benefits.

How Family Can Support You

Throughout your journey to adulthood and through difficulties that you may be facing, one thing is certain: Your family will be there. You need to be able to depend on them emotionally during difficult times. You may just find that they could be the foundation of your emotional structure.

How exactly they will be able to best support you will depend on what you need specifically. You might not be someone who likes speaking about their problems all the time. That's okay, you don't have to. You might be someone who cares for physical affection, but that's okay, too. The important thing is to let them know what they can do to help you.

I know that we often feel like we want to do things by ourselves and for ourselves. That is totally normal, good even. But sometimes you need to sit back and realize that, hey, maybe it's not so bad to let my sibling help me with my to-do list on the day that I feel extra down.

Accepting physical help is just as important as accepting mental health help. In the end, any kind of help that you can receive is for your own benefit. And if it positively impacts you in any way, don't turn it down.

If you're lucky enough to have a good relationship with your parents or with a parent, then you should be grateful for that and ensure that you utilize the support that they will want to offer.

I know it can be annoying when we have "hovering" parents who literally seem to want to follow us everywhere and know about everything. But hey, it is because they love you, and they want to make sure that you know that they are there for you. That's an advantage.

Nothing is quite as scary as a mama bear or a papa bear protecting their cubs. It might be a silly thing to picture, but it does help to know that you've got someone willing to fight for you.

As a parent, I have found that I played a pretty important role in the lives of my kids. Not only because of my experience as a psychologist but because I made sure that they knew I was there for them. And even though they knew that they might get in trouble for certain things, they still spoke to me and asked me for help when they were in a pickle.

Pro tip: Never keep mistakes from your parents. Sure, they might be disappointed, and you might or might not get into a little trouble. Trust me, though, it is much better to have them in your corner and fully clued up on the situation for when the... "mango" hits the fan.

As parents, we would rather be kept in the loop so that we can support and help you during difficult times. You might find yourself in a situation that you do not know how to get out of. But a parent might. And even if they don't, that extra support still helps.

If You Find Yourself in a Dangerous or Unhealthy Situation

Unfortunately, not everyone has positive role models in their lives, and not everyone has the kind of support that they need. In severe cases, things might even get dangerous.

If your trauma might be ongoing, or you find that your home situation is not safe or healthy, it's important to speak out and get the help you need. If you feel unsafe at all, you need to speak up.

Your teachers will likely be equipped to help you in such a case or to get you the help that may be necessary. Never stay silent for the sake of others; your mental and physical health is worth more than that.

In this chapter, we covered a few aspects regarding asking for help, and remember, you're worthy of help!

BONUS CHAPTER

As a bonus, I have decided to add a section with some quotes of positivity to help get you through! I hope that these inspire you as they have inspired me.

These quotes have been taken from various sources and are cited on the reference page.

I also want to share a few success stories so that you know that whatever you're going through can be overcome!

INSPIRATIONAL QUOTES

Confidence is not 'they will like me.' Confidence is 'I'll be fine if they don't.

— CHRISTINA GRIMMIE

Beautiful people are not always good, but good people are always beautiful.

— ALI IBN ABI TALIB

Love yourself. Forgive yourself. Be true to yourself. Because how you treat yourself sets the standard for how others treat you.

— STEVE MARABOLI

You have to be authentic, you have to be true, and you have to believe in your heart.

— HOWARD SCHULTZ

Never bend your head. Always hold it high. Look the world straight in the eye.

— HELLEN KELLER

No matter what you look like or think you look like, you're special, and loved, and perfect just the way you are.

— ARIEL WINTER

Never apologize for being sensitive or emotional. Let this be a sign that you've got a big heart and aren't afraid to let others see it. Showing your emotions is a sign of strength.

— BRIGITTE NICOLE

Everything will be okay in the end. If it's not okay, it's not the end.

— JOHN LENNON

At the end of the day, it's not about what you have or even what you've accomplished. It's about what you've done with those accomplishments. It's about who you've lifted up, who you've made better. It about what you've given back.

— DENZEL WASHINGTON

Learn to enjoy every minute of your life. Be happy now. Don't wait for something outside of yourself to make you happy in the future. Think how really precious is the time you have to spend, whether it's at work or with your family. Every minute should be enjoyed and savored.

— EARL NIGHTINGALE

Success Stories

One of my favorite success stories is not of a celebrity or anyone that you may have heard of. But it's about someone I knew for a very long time and worked with for many years. For the purpose of privacy, no names will be mentioned.

I had a young girl who came from very rough beginnings and was adopted into a good family after traveling through the system for a few years. Her new family was concerned for her, and they did the right thing by seeking professional help for her.

Through intensive therapy and support from her family, the girl became the best version of herself that she could be. Her grades skyrocketed, she finished high school, and she went to college. Today, she is still in college, and hopefully, she'll be a social worker one day.

Her dream is to work with children who have undergone the same kind of trauma that she has and to assist them with rising above where they came from or even their current circumstances.

She went from a frail little girl to a strong, independent woman who is confident in herself and her abilities.

Thoughts

Every success story will be different, and you need to remember that what is considered successful for one is not necessarily for the other. For example, going to college is a great goal and it's absolutely worth it if you're able to do it, but not everyone goes to college, and you can still be successful.

Lady Gaga

One of the most well-known success stories is regarding the one and only Lady Gaga. The popular pop star is known for her immense talent, beauty, and "different" sense of style.

But did you know that she had severe insecurities? In fact, according to the popular magazine "Allure's" issue that was published in 2019, she still has insecurities.

Stefani Germanotta, better known as Lady Gaga, was not an overnight success. It took years of trial and error and hard work for her to finally be discovered. If you know Lady Gaga, you know that she is beautiful. But people didn't always think so; in fact, some record labels actually told her she was not pretty enough (Stibel, 2015).

Through all her hardships and all the backlash she experienced, she never let go of her dream, and even though she felt self-conscious, she kept fighting for what she wanted.

Thoughts

Not everyone is going to like you, but that does not mean that *nobody* will. And it also doesn't mean that you won't make it. It also definitely doesn't mean that you won't get where you want to go. You deserve everything you're dreaming of, and if you work hard enough for it, you'll get it.

Albert Einstein

This next one is absolutely insane; the person we all know as one of the smartest people in history was considered "slow" (Smith & Harte, 2021). I bet you didn't think that the man who literally discovered the general theory of relativity suffered from adversity, eh?

It is likely that if people around him considered him not to be very clever as a child, his self-confidence must have taken a severe dip. Though, in the end, he became one of the most well-known people in history. Even more than 100 years later, most people know who Albert Einstein was.

Thoughts

Other people's perception of you does not define you or your future.

Christina Ricci

Here is another name you've likely heard before. Christina Ricci played the iconic Wednesday Addams in the movies and even got to play a part in the new Wednesday Addams television series. Absolutely known for her stunning looks, the actress hated what she looked like so much that she covered all the mirrors in her house at one point (James, 2016).

To think that the woman, who is one of the most well-known actresses of our time, absolutely could not even stand to look at herself is heartbreaking.

And it kind of puts things into perspective; even celebrities are just people.

Despite how she saw herself, people around the world are in awe of her beauty, and her success is undeniable.

Thoughts

Don't listen to the inner critic; it's often way harder on you than it should be.

Ryan Reynolds

Handsome, successful, loved by many, and completely insecure about himself (Lipson, 2013). According to Ryan, he was very insecure and sensitive as a child and even failed his drama class in school (Rao, 2020).

Today, we know him as many different characters, even the iconic superhero, Deadpool. Despite his insecurities, he flourished.

Thoughts

Fight for what you want, and don't let childhood insecurities get in your way!

If these famous people could all have their own insecurities and adversities yet still reach their dreams and flourish beyond what they initially thought about themselves, then so can you. This list names a few, but there are many. Go ahead and pop a Google search to see how many celebrities actually have or had severe insecurities and issues with self-esteem.

That's the problem with social media; again, these people are portrayed as perfect, but they are just people. Just like us, they have their own issues. We shouldn't try to match up to people who are airbrushed to look and act perfect on camera; it's called "acting" for a reason.

You're enough just the way you are, and no matter how you feel about yourself, you have what it takes.

If you accept and love yourself the way you are and you work hard, there is nothing stopping you from reaching far beyond the stars. And if nobody has told you today, I will; you've got this!

CONCLUSION

The secret to self-confidence isn't to stop caring what people think; it's to start caring about what you think. It's to make your opinion of you more important than anyone else's.

— UNKNOWN

- Your teenage years will throw you in many directions, but guess what? Your whole life awaits you. I hope that this book has empowered you to break free from the cycle of comparison, insecurity, and self-doubt. I hope it encourages you to celebrate your individuality and recognize your inherent worth.

This book has taken us on a journey of self-discovery and empowerment. I have provided what I hope to be invaluable insights into the art of self-love and acceptance, reminding you that you are unique and beautiful just the way you are, no matter what society's standards may say.

To heck with the Barbie and Ken's of the world! Not that looking like Barbie or Ken is a bad thing, but they do kind of represent an "ideal" in regards to looks and acts that we don't need to conform to. Girls don't have to like pink, and boys don't have to like blue! You do you.

We looked at embracing the power of challenging negative thoughts and replacing them with positivity, recognizing that our minds are powerful tools for shaping our reality.

Self-care, a crucial aspect of our well-being, has been emphasized throughout, reminding us to take the time to nurture and nourish ourselves. We've also delved into the importance of mindfulness and acceptance, understanding that there are some things we cannot change, and that's perfectly okay.

Alongside that, we looked at why building healthy relationships is crucial, with a focus on setting boundaries and ensuring our connections are nurturing and respectful. And remember, I also have encouraged you not to be afraid to express yourself and allow your confidence to flourish and your true self to shine.

Finally, we've addressed the challenges of peer pressure and the influence of social media, reminding you that you have the inner strength to stand tall and make choices that are true to your authentic self.

To sum up the main points in a short and concise manner, your seven steps are as follows:

- Don't be bothered by society's standards of beauty or masculinity. They come in many shapes and sizes. Love and accept yourself.
- Challenge your negative thoughts and replace them with more positive ones.
- Self-care is crucial; take care!
- Be mindful, and accept what you cannot change.
- Build healthy relationships, and don't be afraid to set boundaries.

- Don't be afraid to express yourself, and let your confidence grow.
- Peer pressure and social media influences can be tough, but you need to be tougher!

As you close this book, remember that the journey of self-discovery and self-acceptance is ongoing, and each day presents new opportunities to grow, learn, and love yourself a little more. You are resilient, powerful, and capable of embracing your uniqueness and living your best life. You can face whatever challenges come your way.

Your journey toward self-love and empowerment is a lifelong adventure, and you've just taken an important step forward. I'm glad that I got to be a part of this important step.

What are you still sitting down for? Get up and go grab the life you deserve!

The next book in this series will focus on good habits to adopt in the morning for teens... and others.

REFERENCES

Abi-Khalil, T. (2023, July 24). *10 Hollywood actors tith surprising hobbies & side-interests*. ScreenRant. https://screenrant.com/movie-actors-surprising-hobby-side-interest/

Alder, S. (n.d.). *Shanon L. Alder quotes*. Goodreads. https://www.goodreads.com/quotes/6183934-confidence-is-knowing-who-you-are-and-not-changing-it

American Psychological Association. (2022). *Mindfulness*. Apa.org. https://www.apa.org/topics/mindfulness#:~:text=Mindfulness%20is%20awareness%20of%20one

Anonymous. (n.d.). *Anonymous quotes*. Quotefancy. https://quotefancy.com/quote/756898/Anony

mous-I-m-too-busy-working-on-my-own-grass-to-notice-if-yours-is-greener

Bierig, S. (n.d.). *Sandra Bierig quotes*. Best Positive Quotes. https://bestpositivequotes.com/author/sandra-bierig/to-accept-ourselves-as-we-are-means-to-value-our-imperfections-as

Body image: What is it, and how can I improve it? (2020, September 16). Www.medicalnewstoday.com. https://www.medicalnewstoday.com/articles/249190#:~:text=A%20body%20image%20does%20not

Capecchi, S. (2022, June 8). *Mindfulness for teens: How it works, benefits, & 11 exercises to try*. Choosing Therapy. https://www.choosingtherapy.com/mindfulness-for-teens/

Casabianca, S. S. (2021, May 6). *15 cognitive distortions to blame for your negative thinking*. Psych Central. https://psychcentral.com/lib/cognitive-distortions-negative-thinking#list-and-examples

CDC. (2020, September 10). *Sleep in middle and high school students*. Www.cdc.gov. https://www.cdc.gov/healthyschools/features/students-sleep.htm#:~:text=Importance%20of%20Sleep&text=The%20American%20Academy%20of%20Sleep

Cherney, K. (2020, August 25). *Effects of anxiety on the body*. Healthline. https://www.healthline.com/health/anxiety/effects-on-body

Cicero, M T. (n.d.). *Marcus Tullius Cicero quotes*. Goodreads. https://www.goodreads.com/quotes/1186941-if-you-have-no-confidence-in-yourself-you-are-twice

Cuncic, A. (2020, June 29). *How to change your negative thought patterns when you have SAD*. Verywell Mind. https://www.verywellmind.com/how-to-change-negative-thinking-3024843

Dokmak, A. (n.d.). *Asmaa Dokmak quotes*. Goodreads. https://goodreads.com/quotes/9898305-to-build-self-esteen-you-have-to-outface-your-negative-beliefs

DeGeneres, E. (n.d.). *Ellen DeGeneres quotes*. Quotefancy. https://www.quotefancy.com/quote/801826/Ellen-DeGeneres-The-most-important-thing-in-your-life-is-to-live-your-likfe-with-integrity

Dr. Seuss. (n.d.). *Dr. Seuss quotes*. Goodreads. https://www.goodreads.com/quotes/187115-why-fit-in-when-you-were-born-to-stand-out

Drury, J. (2019, December 24). *Do these 5 things to maintain healthy perspective.* The CEO Magazine. https://www.theceomagazine.com/business/health-wellbeing/5-things-to-maintain-healthy-perspective/

50+ Inspirational quotes for teens. (2020, August 27). Thought Catalog. https://thoughtcatalog.com/january-nelson/2020/08/inspirational-quotes-for-teens/

Fleming, W. (2022, June 20). *50+ Awesome and inspirational quotes for teenagers.* Parentingteensandtweens.com. https://parentingteensandtweens.com/inspirational-quotes-for-teenagers/

Grimmie, C. (n.d.). Christiana Grimmie quotes. Goodreads. https://www.goodreads.com/quotes/5826874-confidence-is-not-they-will-like-me-confidence-instead-is

Hall, L. (2022, February 25). *Boost your confidence with these uplifting quotes.* Country Living. https://www.countryliving.com/life/inspirational-stories/a39116740/confidence-quotes/

Hopper, C. (2018, March 30). *160+ inspirational quotes for teens to encourage them.* Skip to My Lou. https://

www.skiptomylou.org/inspirational-quotes-for-teens/

James, C. (2016, November 29). *15 celebs you didn't know struggled with low self-esteem*. TheTalko. https://www.thetalko.com/15-celebs-you-didnt-know-struggled-with-low-self-esteem/

Julie. (2022, September 2). *125 motivational quotes for teens to encourage & inspire*. More than Main Street. https://www.morethanmainstreet.com/motivational-quotes-for-teens/

Juma, N. (2017, December). *Inspirational quotes for kids about peer pressure*. Everyday Power. https://everydaypower.com/peer-pressure-quotes/

Keller, H. (n.d.). Helen Keller quotes. Brainyquote. https://www.brainyquote.com/quotes/helen_keller_162480

Kishore, K. (2020, October 2). *What Is peer pressure? How does it influence you?* Harappa. https://harappa.education/harappa-diaries/what-is-peer-pressure-and-its-examples/#:~:text=Peer%20influence%20is%20the%20pressure,especially%20during%20our%20growing%20years.

Lady Gaga: A profile in failure. (2015). Linkedin.com. https://www.linkedin.com/pulse/lady-gaga-profile-failure-jeff-stibel

Lennon, J. (n.d.). *John Lennon quotes.* Goodreads. https://www.goodreads.com/quotes/628927-every thing-will-be-okay-in-the-end-if-it-s-not

Lipson, D. (2013, October 9). *20 celebs you'd never guess are insecure.* HuffPost. https://www.huffpost. com/entry/insecure-stars_n_4072312

LPC, J. E., MS. (2014, February 5). *Connection between mindfulness and body image.* Eating Disorder Hope. https://www.eatingdisorderhope.com/blog/mindful ness-can-help-improve-body-image

Maraboli, S. (n.d.). *Steve Maraboli quotes.* Goodreads. https://www.goodreads.com/quotes/695646-love-yourself-forgive-yourself-be-true-to-yourself-how-you

Martin, S. (2017, January 30). *16 quotes to inspire healthy relationships.* Psych Central. https://psychcen tral.com/blog/imperfect/2017/01/16-quotes-to-inspire-healthy-relationships#Quotes-to-Inspire-Healthy-Relationships:

Martino, A. (2021, April 13). *Creative outlets importance and benefits*. Global Talent Link. https://www.gtlink.us/the-importance-and-benefits-of-creative-outlets/#:~:text=Research%20has%20shown%20that%20during

Mayo Clinic staff. (2022, December 13). *Body dysmorphic disorder - Symptoms and causes*. Mayo Clinic. https://www.mayoclinic.org/diseases-conditions/body-dysmorphic-disorder/symptoms-causes/syc-20353938

McCarthy, K., McCarthy, M. E. K., educator, M. E. A. a fomer, Four, M. B. W. a M. of, tips, K. shares helpful, & Policy, advice on a variety of topics R. M. L. about our E. (n.d.). *85 Self-confidence quotes to inspire belief in yourself*. LoveToKnow. Retrieved September 12, 2023, from https://www.lovetoknow.com/quotes-quips/inspirational/85-self-confidence-quotes-inspire-belief-yourself

McLeod, N. S. (2023, October 1). *Bad bitch quotes to inspire confidence within you*. Everyday Power. https://everydaypower.com/bad-bitch-quotes/

Monroe, M. (n.d.). *Marilyn Monroe quotes*. BrainyQuote. https://brainyquote.com/quotes/marilyn_monroe_498577

Nawab, A. (2023, July 7). *The unusual hobbies of 9 famous celebrities.* MangoBaaz. https://www.mangobaaz.com/the-unusual-hobbies-of-9-famous-celebrities

Nicole, B. (n.d.). *Brigitte Nicole quotes.* Goodreads. https://www.goodreads.com/quotes/1007979-never-apolgize-for-being-sensitive-or-emotional-let-this-be

Nicole, S. (n.d.). *Solange Nicole quotes.* Goodreads. https://www.goodreads.com/quotes/462333-a-diamond-doesn-t-start-out-polished-and-shining-it-once

Nightingale, E. (n.d.). *Earl Nightingale quotes.* Brainyquote. https://www.brainyquote.com/quotes/earl_nightingale_159029

Negative thinking quotes (107 quotes). (n.d.). Goodreads. https://www.goodreads.com/quotes/tag/negative-thinking

Olsen, M. (n.d.). *Mary-Kate Olsen quotes.* Quotefancy. https://www.quotefancy.com/quote/1352016/Mary-Kate-Olsen-I-think-the-hardest-part-to-get-to-is-that-point-of-asking-for-help-or

Outreach. (2021, November 19). *Negative thought patterns and depression*. Sage Neuroscience Center. https://sageclinic.org/blog/negative-thoughts-depression/

Peer pressure quotes (113 quotes). (2011). Goodreads. https://www.goodreads.com/quotes/tag/peer-pressure

Rao, M. (2020, July 20). *How Ryan Reynolds used his insecurities to propel himself to stardom*. Medium. https://mannyrao.medium.com/how-ryan-reynolds-used-his-insecurities-to-propel-himself-to-stardom-7dd72213f720

Scott, E. (2022, May 24). *The toxic effects of negative self-talk*. Verywell Mind. https://www.verywellmind.com/negative-self-talk-and-how-it-affects-us-4161304

Self-care Quotes: Definition and examples. (n.d.). The Berkeley Well-Being Institute. https://www.berkeleywellbeing.com/self-care-quotes.html

Shultz, H. (n.d.). Howard Shultz quotes. Quotecatalogue. https://www.quotecatalogue.com/quote/howard-shultz-you-have-to-be-72mg921

Smith, R., & Harte, V. (2021, June 28). *10 famous people who raised their self-esteem*. Dummies. https://www.dummies.com/article/body-mind-spirit/emotional-health-psychology/emotional-health/general-emotional-health/10-famous-people-who-raised-their-self-esteem-145436/

Stibel, J. (2015). *Lady Gaga: A profile in failure*. Linkedin.com. https://www.linkedin.com/pulse/lady-gaga-profile-failure-jeff-stibel

Talib, A. (n.d.). Ali ibn Abi Talib quotes. Quotefancy. https://www.quotefancy.com/quote/1439312/Ali-ibn-Abi-Talib-Beautiful-people-are-not-always-good-but-good-people-are-always

The 50 best quotes on self-love. (n.d.). Psychologytoday. Retrieved September 12, 2023, from https://www.psychologytoday.com/za/blog/the-mindful-self-express/201210/the-50-best-quotes-self-love

The Rock reveals his personal struggle to feel confident. (2019, April 30). Men's Health. https://www.menshealth.com/entertainment/a27319726/the-rock-confidence-instagram-video/

TOP 25 ASKING FOR HELP QUOTES. (n.d.). A-Z Quotes. https://www.azquotes.com/quotes/topics/asking-for-help.html

TOP 25 PEER PRESSURE QUOTES (of 90). (n.d.). A-Z Quotes. https://www.azquotes.com/quotes/topics/peer-pressure.html

TOP 25 SELF CONSCIOUS QUOTES (of 356). (n.d.). A-Z Quotes. Retrieved September 10, 2023, from https://www.azquotes.com/quotes/topics/self-conscious.html#:~:text=Once%20you%20become%20self%2Dconscious

Tort-Nasarre, G., Pollina Pocallet, M., & Artigues-Barberà, E. (2021). The meaning and factors that influence the concept of body image: Systematic review and meta-ethnography from the perspectives of adolescents. *International Journal of Environmental Research and Public Health, 18*(3), 1140. https://doi.org/10.3390/ijerph18031140

Washington, D. (n.d.). *Denzel Washington quotes*. Goodreads. https://www.goodreads.com/quotes/413356-at-the-end-of-the-day-it-s-not-about-what

West, K. (n.d.). *Kanye West quotes*. Quotefancy. https://www.quotefancy.com/quote/1465461/Kanye-West-Yeah-I-think-that-I-have-like-faltered-you-know-as-a-human-my-message-isn-t

Williams, R. (n.d.). *Robin Williams quotes*. https://brainyquote.com/quotes/robin_williams_650958

Winter, A. (n.d.). Ariel Winter quotes. Quotefancy. https://www.quotefancy.com/quote/1617198-Ariel-Winter-No-matter-what-you-look-like-or-think-you-look-like-you-re-special-and-loved

youth.gov. (n.d.). *Characteristics of healthy & unhealthy relationships* . Youth.gov. https://youth.gov/youth-topics/teen-dating-violence/characteristics

Zendaya Quotes. (n.d.). BrainyQuote. https://www.brainyquote.com/authors/zendaya-quotes

A SPECIAL THANK YOU!

Thank you for supporting me and reading this book! I hope that the journey has been a fruitful one and that you enjoyed reading it as much as I enjoyed writing it! May all your future travels be successful and joyous!

You can help me by leaving a review! This helps me with writing more books that you will love. I would love to hear from you as well.

Thank you again for purchasing this book!